PRAISE FOR

Roots and Wings

"Margery is an extraordinary woman who's making a positive, lasting impact and building a better world . . . She teaches us how she nurtured a beautiful, active and engaged family while creating, building and running a groundbreaking company."

—SYLVIA BURWELL, President, American University (2017–present); Secretary, US Department of Health and Human Services (2014–2017); Director, US Office of Management and Budget (2013–2014)

"Margery is a transformational leader who has proven that one can be brilliant, decent, and forward-thinking in life generally and specifically in building a company that helps to prove that one can do well by doing good."

—DANIEL GLICKMAN, Chairman and CEO, Motion Picture Association of America (2004–2010); Secretary, US Department of Agriculture (1995–2001); US Congressman, Kansas 4th Congressional District (1977–1995)

"Through real-life examples, Margery illustrates how being a good business leader makes us better parents and how good parenting delivers an invaluable skillset to the workplace. Rather than competing, the two goals work together to weave a tapestry that is both stronger and more beautiful than they are alone."

—LINDA MCMAHON, 25th Administrator, US Small Business Administration (2017–2019); Co-founder and Chief Executive Officer of World Wrestling Entertainment (1982–2009)

ROOTS
AND
WINGS

ROOTS
AND
WINGS

TEN LESSONS
OF MOTHERHOOD
THAT HELPED ME
CREATE AND RUN
A COMPANY

by

MARGERY KRAUS

with Phyllis J. Piano

Published by SparkPress, a BookSparks imprint,
A division of SparkPoint Studio, LLC
Phoenix, Arizona, USA, 85007
www.gosparkpress.com

Published 2019
Printed in the United States of America
ISBN: 978-1-68463-024-0 (pbk)
ISBN: 978-1-68463-025-7 (e-bk)

Library of Congress Control Number: 2019942905

Book design by Stacey Aaronson

For my family, at home and at work . . .

CONTENTS

ROOTS
AND
WINGS

PREFACE

WHY write a book?

Over the years, many people have encouraged me to share the experiences I have had building my company. I just never felt the time was right . . . and still am not quite there for that kind of book. But when the chance came up to think about what I have learned from my private life that has enabled me to provide a framework to my business life and talk about my personal passions, I was not only intrigued by the idea, but it also felt right to share that part of the journey in the hope that it would help others sort through their own journey.

During the past few years, through my company, APCO Worldwide, I have spent a lot of time in companies with their leaders talking about purpose—why are they in business and what is really important to them? Helping clients articulate "meaning" and "purpose" has been an important part of our work in today's environment. I realized that all this focus on purpose is also relevant to our personal lives. And, as I have gotten older, I have spent more time thinking about personal purpose . . . what makes your life relevant and fulfilled and what do you leave behind?

As I have thought about it, I have realized that my personal passions and my work are as intertwined as the stories I tell in the pages that follow about my family and my company. I have always felt that job one was being a good wife, mother, and grandmother. But I have also been blessed with the opportunity to create an extended family of hundreds of others from around the world who have become part of an intimate circle of importance to me—staff I have mentored, clients I have served, and friends I have made along the way.

So when I started my business—I was already thirty-eight and my kids were in junior high or high school—I made a pledge. 1) I didn't care how big the business would become, I just wanted it to be significant, to make a difference in the lives of our clients and staff, and wherever possible, to take on challenges that could help shape a better world. 2) I wanted to work with smart people who were also nice and decent and liked to work together for the common interests of the firm, not for their own self-importance. 3) I wanted the company to be bound by a common culture that superseded nationality, political leanings, or other traditional groups.

While I didn't realize it at the time, it was APCO's purpose to bring together some of the smartest (and nicest) people in their respective fields to create opportunities or solve problems that bring value to our clients and, wherever possible, use the platform created to contribute to a better world. It was my hope that creating this environment and the culture that supported it would provide a career of fulfillment (at least at the professional level) to our people.

I honestly believe this purpose was shared with my view of family. I am a passionate but honest advocate for my children and grandchildren. I have tried my best to provide a stimulating, safe, and loving environment where family values are clear (roots) but paths to happiness are multiple (wings).

I am very proud of the role models my kids and their kids have turned out to be. I like to think, looking back, that this is a great legacy and one that gives significance and meaning to my time on earth.

More than anything, both environments are bound by mutual respect, curiosity, honesty, and hard work. And my life's motto is to "think big and have passion."

—Margery Kraus

Work/Family Balance: Can You Have It All?

THE question of how to achieve the perfect balance between work and family is a difficult one. Many believe there is no such thing. Being torn between the demands of work and the pull of family obligations leaves many frustrated and exhausted. How can you do the best job at both? It is a question I have been asked hundreds of times over my career as each new generation tries to find the right answer.

I can only tell you what I have done. The answer for me has been blending the two, so this book is about the convergence of work and personal life. In many ways, my professional success has been a function of a supportive and engaged family, and my ability to be fully engaged with my family has been a function of a fulfilled professional career. It hasn't always been easy, but it has worked for me, and I hope these personal experiences can give others ideas about how to make this difficult balance work for them.

When it comes to work and family balance, everybody has to have their own formula. The way I've done it is not for everyone. My advice is to find your own way and go in with your eyes open.

I come from a generation where it was a given that if I was going to have a career, it was on me. Not that I would do it all by myself; I just couldn't complain about it. No one was telling me to find a job and work outside the home.

One thing I learned early on was to be in the present. What I mean by that is my model of work and life integration didn't allow me to carry all my work home and all my problems to work. The second thing that became clear was that I needed to have a really secure spouse and we had to be in agreement on how everything was going to work. Believe me, it took a while for us to adjust, but we agreed it was a partnership that all of us—kids included—would participate in, pitching in. This made all the difference in the world, giving me such a strong support system.

As the kids grew up, they did sacrifice certain things. I didn't drive carpools—my husband did that more—and I traveled and wasn't always there to help with their schoolwork or be there for them.

My kids were treated with a level of responsibility and accountability for things at home, which was a necessity for me as a working mom. The kids had to help around the house, which they may have found very difficult or unfair, given their peers most likely had a mom at home. As they went to college and became adults, they really appreciated their responsibilities because they all learned to take care of themselves and work together as a team to get things done for the family. If I did not have that level of support from them, my career would have been impossible.

Listen, I don't want to make it sound too perfect. There

were days that I just wanted to pull my hair out. I didn't know how I was going to get through it, as it seemed like everything was going wrong.

One particular incident that still haunts me was the day my oldest daughter, Lisa, then about seven or eight, was riding her bike in the neighborhood and got her pants caught in the chain and fell. She was stuck and just lying on the side of the road (we lived on a cul-de-sac, so she was in no danger) until someone saw her and helped her. I was mortified by the thought of my daughter on that street and her mother too far away to help! In retrospect, it wasn't a big thing, but all working mothers experience something that makes us feel guilty and question our priorities. There is no reason to think that I would have known about this to help any sooner if I were home, but this incident is the kind of thing that would set off any mother trying to balance things and worried about doing everything well.

The societal norms at that time would label me a bad mother, and some school staff and acquaintances would even *tell* my kids I was a bad mother. It was so upsetting. But on balance, all of us had to work through those things. Communication was key in getting the kids to understand that I was not leaving them, but doing something important for everyone's benefit. And having a husband who was a helpmate made the hard days easier.

It was gratifying to me that my children were very proud when they would go with me to work and see what I did. I believe this experience made them aspire to do great things in their lives.

Interestingly, I didn't necessarily plan to have a career, at least not right away. I grew up in a small town where my family had a general store. While the family was well known in our town of three thousand people, they were immigrants. My father immigrated to the US from Poland when he was a toddler, and his family settled in a small mining town in New Jersey called Franklin, where his father became the town baker. After serving in World War II, my father started a surplus store that evolved into a small department store called Safer Trading Company.

My mother was also born in Poland, but she was raised in Cuba because her family could not get papers to come to the United States. They were also bakers, and my mother and father met on a date arranged by their parents, who had become acquainted when my father's parents were in Cuba on holiday.

Because we owned the town general store (more of a mini department store), all of us kids worked from the time we could remember. The store was open twelve hours a day, six days a week, so we all did our part to help our parents. It was a gathering point for the community, and I learned the power of trusted relationships early, as my father often gave needed credit on a handshake and people never let him down.

My mother often worked in the store as well, leaving to go home to cook dinner and make sure we did our homework and took care of the house. I never really thought of her as a working mom, although, in retrospect, she really had to balance a lot of things. She was very traditional in lots of ways, given her Cuban upbringing and her deference to her husband, whom she adored.

Later in life, my parents would divorce, sell the store, and move on to separate lives, but I was already through college and finding my own path. More on this later.

I have always worked hard and dreamed big. Since my school in Franklin was K–12 in one building, I decided to go to college early and left high school after my junior year to enroll at Knox College in Galesburg, Illinois. (While it was highly unusual for colleges to accept students after their junior year of high school and it was not a common practice, some colleges did if they were satisfied with the student's grades and test scores were sufficiently compelling.) Many people—my family included—thought that I would go on to do great things, so it was a big surprise when I announced my engagement at age nineteen and our plans to marry the next summer, even before I had finished college.

I married Steve Kraus, a Brooklyn boy who was just finishing law school in Washington, DC. Steve was from a close-knit but very traditional family. I am not sure anyone anticipated that I would look to have a career. At least, it was never discussed. So I finished school, taught for a short time, and had our first child, Lisa. I had thought that when our kids were older, I would follow Steve, go to law school, and perhaps pursue a legal career. To keep my mind alert, I decided to go to graduate school at night, a move my husband fully supported.

What happened next changed everything. Throughout my life, I have always taken on more than perhaps was a reasonable amount of things to juggle. Yet I had always worked hard, so I didn't mind putting in the effort. And I have always been a sucker for a good opportunity and get easily seduced by things that I believe make a difference.

After having my first child and enrolling in graduate school, I had an opportunity to take on an assignment—a full-time job—for the next six months. I decided it was really something I wanted to do but had no idea how I would pull it off. It required keeping up with household duties, caring for a six-month-old, and going to graduate school while taking on this short-term but full-time job with a start-up educational program using Washington as a classroom—something in which I believed strongly as both a political scientist and teacher. I went from being a stay-at-home mother to trying to balance a trifecta of work, school, and motherhood—all within a relatively new marriage to someone who didn't sign up for this bargain.

But I was stubborn and wanted to try. I won't go into the details of that intense schedule of full but fulfilling days, but I will share some of the lessons learned. And yes, I survived, my child survived, and our marriage survived for the next fifty-two years. And we are still going strong after a half century.

In order for me to pursue this opportunity, I had to have a true partnership with my husband, who is a lawyer and had his own career. It was the late 60s, and this was very unconventional. For both of us, it took effort and patience. Over time, we learned how to be true partners to balance our family and work lives. Without this type of unconditional love and buy-in at home, it is difficult for women and men to have any type of work/family balance. This equilibrium is essential. We've been fortunate to find a formula that works for us.

One of the side benefits of my having a career is that, over the years, my husband got to develop a special relationship with his children that men of his age rarely got to do. He became a role model of a different kind as well. My husband has gotten a lot of joy out of that special relationship with the children. As the kids grew and watched us as a couple, they looked to us for different things but respected us as individuals, which has been an important aspect of the health of our family.

I learned a lot from my early experiences. I learned to be down-to-earth and approachable. It's hard not to be when, particularly in the early years, I'd go home, make dinner, do the wash, scrub the floors . . . I learned to have empathy for staff as they try to juggle it all, and I endeavor to give each of my employees the flexibility they need to manage their work and family lives, understanding that each situation is unique. It's easier for me to understand what they face because I experienced the push and pull of work and family as a young working mother. I learned the importance of being able to multitask and use time efficiently. I also learned the valuable lesson of sharing your difficulties and your joys with those at home who support you.

When I started my company, I resolved to involve my kids in my work. Now, you might say it was easier for me to do that since it is my company. While you may be right, there are thousands of ways to involve your kids (and grandkids) in what you do for work.

I attended *Fortune*'s Most Powerful Women Summit a few years ago, and one of the speakers, a J.P. Morgan Chase executive, talked about how she blends work and family. For her executive job, she travels the world and then goes home and spins the globe to show her children the countries to which she's been and describes the people she's met, the different cultures, and the problems she seeks to address. She also uses the currencies for a math lesson. On the surface, it may seem difficult to relate international finance to children, but it can be done, and her children are better for it.

Just about any job has multiple aspects that could be made of interest to kids. Challenge yourself, and, believe me, the children can surprise you as well. I never thought my granddaughter Brennan would take an interest in Italian politics, but she did, getting into intense discussions with the staff in Rome while I was in a meeting. The pride I felt as this ten-year-old asked insightful questions of the Italian staff was the thing I remembered most about that trip, and it is a memory that she and I will always share. It also made quite an impression on the Italian staff that I was traveling with my granddaughter, who was so interested in what I did.

So in answer to the question about work/family balance, I believe that it does not exist. The only way I've found to "have it all" is to *blend* work and family, enriching all.

I founded my company in 1984. I have traveled the

world many times over, averaging about forty trips and close to a half million miles per year. I have been married for fifty-two years, and we have three children and nine grandchildren. When my children were young, I created the "ten-year-old trip," first for my kids and now for my grandchildren. This has been an important part of the work/family integration because it both exposes the kids to a world beyond home and gives them a window into my life of work. When they reach their tenth birthday, I travel with the birthday boy or girl to the place they choose in the world (often involving an APCO office), and they have to do intensive research and explain the choice. Generally, the research starts about a year in advance. The trip to Rome I described was a part of Brennan's (my third granddaughter) ten-year-old trip.

I probably could write a separate book about all of these trip experiences—seven so far, with two grandkids to go. I've learned many lessons—they have too—and I will sprinkle these throughout the book, as well as some comments from my children and grandchildren. We have all learned so much together.

I don't mean to imply that I am a perfect mother or leader—far from it—but I've learned much over the years and have taken the lessons from motherhood and applied them to my work and vice versa. I hope there is something helpful for you in what I've learned so far.

Margery's mother, Lily Cvern, as a young woman.

*Margery's mother, Lily Cvern, leaving Cuba for a new life
in the United States in 1941.*

Margery's paternal grandfather, Meyer Rosen, with his bakery truck in Franklin, New Jersey, circa 1940.

Margery's parents, Lily and Sol Rosen, on their wedding day, April 17, 1943.

Margery and her father were very close from her earliest days.

Margery, her parents, and brother, Bob,
celebrating her brother's fourth birthday in 1948.

Margery and Steve Kraus on their wedding day,
September 4, 1966, in Brooklyn, New York.

Steve and Margery Kraus on their honeymoon in Puerto Rico
following their wedding in 1966.

Steve's parents, Evelyn and Benjamin Kraus, with Margery and Steve's oldest daughter, Lisa, and son, Evan, in 1971.

CHAPTER ONE

Lesson One:
Give Them Roots and Wings

"The greatest gifts you can give your children are the roots of responsibility and the wings of independence."
—DENIS WAITLEY

ALMOST since the beginning of parenthood, I had a little sign in my house that read, "The only lasting thing of value you give your children is roots and wings." It always struck me that these words were a great guidepost for raising my kids. It later became the underlying philosophy that guided the spirit and culture of my company.

As parents, we try to create the most stable and supportive environment for our children so their roots are strong and they have a clear understanding of some basic values that guide the family: respect for each other, telling the truth, working hard, keeping your word, and a sense of modesty and fair play, among other things. If these values are embraced and become part of their DNA, you know your children can accept the responsibilities of freedom because they will make good choices and stay true to their roots.

We can then look forward to the day that they earn their independence and "wings" as we watch them grow and develop into passionate and productive members of society and trust them to find their own way. We always want them to be safe, happy, and fulfilled, so it can be tricky to know when to let them fly free. It's easy to be overprotective and try to make decisions for them or have rules that make no sense.

If we've given our children strong roots and done our best to help them develop to their fullest potential, we step back to let them try out their wings to succeed and fail on their own. We can pick them up when they fall and encourage them to get back out there, but they gain experience through these lessons learned.

These roots—an understanding of what is expected and what is appropriate and valued, coupled with the faith and trust that comes with the freedom to make decisions—are more than a parent's love or pride. It is what builds self-confidence and fuels personal achievement. If your children are instilled with the right values, then you can give them responsibility for their own decisions and let them fly.

In my own family, we had rules and responsibilities. But we also gave our children a lot of freedom to make their own choices—freedom within a framework, so to speak. Growing up, my parents gave us a lot of responsibility. When we were only teenagers, my older brother and I were sometimes responsible for running the store, including closing out the register, waiting on customers, dealing with wholesalers, and other aspects of the business. At the same time, we were given a lot of freedom regarding where we wanted to go, whom we wanted to date, curfews, and other things important to teenagers. We had that freedom as long as we didn't abuse it. It was on us, and the fear of abusing that trust was a stronger incentive to stay the course than any punishment that could have been inflicted.

My husband and I tried to do the same thing with our kids. Since I was always working, they took a lot of responsibility at home: the older for the younger, chores, some cooking, and various other things. There was an inherent trust that they would do the right thing, and if and when that trust was violated, they helped determine the appropriate punishment that fit the "crime."

I sometimes wonder if this put too much pressure on our oldest, as she assumed a lot of responsibility for her siblings early in life. She would often critique the variety of housekeepers/babysitters we had, saying that she ended up taking the responsibility and figuring out how to handle things and then we would pay the housekeeper! There were many times she was right and exercised more common sense than the rest of us.

We all had role models that reinforced this approach to life. Mine was my Uncle Sammy. He influenced me more than anyone during my formative years and became my most important hero, even if I didn't know it at the time. Sammy was a loving person, a great athlete, and, really, my idol. He was my mother's youngest brother and was closer in age to us than her. While his parents were still in Cuba, he came to the US and lived with us and was kind of a big brother to me. Sammy had a great personality and was loved by all. He balanced his wit with his wisdom and taught me to live life to its fullest and make each day count.

When he developed cancer in his spine at age twenty-one, I was devastated, but he handled adversity with dignity and courage and taught me to never be afraid of anything. I sat with him every day for five months until he died. Watching him face death and pass on was very hard for me as a fourteen-year-old, but being with him until the end taught me a lot. Perhaps this experience early in my life gave me the courage to take risks, to be bold, as I understood at a young age how fragile life was and how much we take for granted. I always thought if I died when I was twenty-one, I wanted to die happy, having done great things and gone for it, never holding back. I still miss Uncle Sammy. I wish he could see who I am now, my family, and what I've done. I know he'd be really proud.

Maybe Uncle Sammy pushed me to achieve and make a difference, as life can be so short. I don't know, but I am so grateful to have had him in my life, with our relationship an important part of my roots. And your personal roots are the beginning of your professional ones; they blend together over time.

As I mentioned before, I got my first taste of the workplace when I was a teenager in the 60s. In business, I learned so many lessons and gained excellent experience working in my dad's store. Working in retail sales is a great training ground, and my brother and I learned a lot about personal responsibility and customer service and satisfaction during our years at the store.

Everyone in our small town had a story about my dad. He ran a business and we had a good living, but he didn't run it at the expense of others. He ran it with passion and humanity. Our town was a mining town and not a very wealthy place. People often lived paycheck to paycheck and sometimes didn't have the extra cash to buy that special present or, in one case, the engagement ring a customer needed to ask his future bride for her hand in marriage. There were no credit cards—all that would come later, long after I was gone from the town and the store. My dad would keep an open tab for his customers to help them through these moments. They would pay what they could and settle the rest over time. He developed a lot of loyalty among his customers, and the store became a gathering place and a central part of the community.

This taught me the value of trusted relationships in business. Living your personal values in your work pays dividends and creates a sense of satisfaction that is often lost today. I have tried to instill this in my own business but learned it can also lead to disappointments when you are dealing with people who don't share the same values, as I learned with the first investors in my business. That was a tough lesson for me, but it reinforced the importance of shared values as a common basis for creating a work culture and work ethic.

My father also owned a semi-professional football team

called the Franklin Miners. This team was originally formed from the mine workers in Franklin, New Jersey, who played on weekends for recreation. My father outfitted the team from his store and announced the games. When the mines closed in 1955, he took over the team and built it into the best semi-pro team in the US.

Football became part of our life, and the stories of being a young woman traveling with a semi-pro football team could fill a book and helped prepare me for just about anything in life. It felt a little bit like the Wild West. I learned how to dance between raindrops—when to be tough and when not to be—and how to handle myself in a variety of difficult circumstances. It also taught me that when there are no shared values or ethics, you sometimes have to act or be proactive to protect yourself.

In traveling with my dad in the world of semi-pro football—and being from a small town—I learned that not everyone shares your values. The team used to play for gate receipts—the money that was collected for admission to the game—and these funds supported the players. Inevitably, when it looked like our team would win, there would be a problem locating the gate receipts or they would detain my father and find an excuse to take the money back. After being burned once or twice, my dad came up with an idea. If he gave those receipts to me, it was unlikely anyone would bother questioning his teenage daughter! It worked, and we had many tales to share that bonded us forever.

My first job out of college was as a high school civics teacher—a job I did for a short time before having my first child. It's amazing how much one can learn about life—both triumph and tragedy—from teaching teenagers. Working with high school students definitely gives you a mirror on society at large. There were the stars, of course, the self-motivated students who give you great pleasure. But I also saw the impact of kids whose self-confidence, personal image, motivation, and aspirations were totally different. I came to understand how the formation of strong roots influences life choices.

My time in the classroom made me believe more than ever in the importance of personal experience in shaping education and self-esteem, which pushed me to take on assignments that led to my role in the formation of the Close Up Foundation, a job that challenged me to put to use my belief in using education to change lives.

I had heard that Close Up was starting, and I knew this was exactly what I wanted to do. I felt passionate about using Washington as a classroom, and I finished my degree at American University doing just that. I felt like I had these insights that could be very useful and there weren't that many people with this exact experience. I went in to talk to the people who were starting Close Up and gave them a bunch of ideas. They had planned to start the program in about a month and appreciated my insights but didn't have any money to hire me, as they were operating on a shoestring. I offered them a money-back guarantee. I told them, "I really want to do this. Hire me, and you don't have to pay me unless it works." And I got the job, obviously.

What was supposed to be a five-week assignment

turned into fourteen years. If you decide you want to do something you are passionate about, you just have to go for it.

Again, this was a hard choice because it was a tipping point in my career. I was making a decision to go from an occasional assignment while finishing graduate school to having a full-time or more-than-full-time job. And with that came all the anxiety of being a working mother and the concerns about whether my personal passion for the work I was taking on was selfish. It's not that we didn't need the money, but that was not the primary consideration. I really believed in the mission of the foundation and thought I could make a difference. But I also had important responsibilities at home, and this was the beginning of work/life integration for me.

Close Up put me, a girl from Franklin, New Jersey, in front of some of the most important leaders of this country, and along with the students, I met and worked with four different presidents (Ford, Carter, Reagan, and Clinton). There were several trips to the Oval Office or the Rose Garden with the Close Up students, and Lisa—and then her brother Evan when he was of age—were always part of this.

Lisa participated from the time she was in first grade. In fact, there is a very funny story about Lisa going to the Oval Office to meet President Ford. She told her teacher that she was not going to be in school the next day because she was going to the White House to meet the president. The teacher actually punished her, thinking she was making up a story. The day after her visit, by chance, she appeared on the front page of the Grand Rapids, Michigan, newspaper, greeting President Ford. I took great delight in sending the paper to school with Lisa the following day.

I had a wonderful career at Close Up. This superb organization has a mission to inform, inspire, and empower young people to exercise the rights and accept the responsibilities of citizens in a democracy. I passionately embraced their mission and loved what I did every day. Close Up gave me so many experiences and enriched my life, deepening my working roots. As a result, I knew what I wanted to do professionally.

While Close Up's mission sounds very US focused, it actually wasn't, as it opened my eyes to the important role the US plays in the world and made me think globally in everything I did. As a result, to this day, I constantly think about how I can connect people in ways so they get things done that make the world better.

I was happy at Close Up and really didn't think about moving on. But as I have learned in life, good opportunities don't always appear at convenient times or in expected ways. As part of Close Up, I had the good fortune to work with Dr. Howard Mehlinger, who was, at the time, a guru in social studies education. He became a good friend and mentor to me as I was building Close Up and wanted to ensure it had the educational rigor to make a difference.

Howard was a professor at Indiana University and was appointed to head a task force on the bicentennial of the constitution and, as part of that effort, took on a project to update the European textbooks and their treatment of teaching about the United States. He appointed a small group to spend part of the summer of 1983 with him in Hamburg, Germany, where the master teachers assembled. While the small group of Americans asked to participate were all noted academics, Howard thought my participation, both as the only woman and as a non-academic with lots of practical experience and stories from my Close Up experience, would add something to the group.

It was a remarkable experience in many ways and left me with life lessons about prejudice, friendships, the unique role women play at times, and a love for the experience of living someone else's culture. It also introduced me to Arnold & Porter (A&P), as the law firm was counsel to this commission.

The group of partners at A&P who were involved were extremely creative and often got involved in major projects with non-legal professionals—almost as often as they were practicing law. As they learned more about Close Up and what I was doing, they became more interested, particularly in the way Close Up had partnered with C-SPAN in using downtime on their satellite to take Washington into classrooms via cable.

Their interest in the Close Up programs on cable, combined with the exposure from the task force, led to a surprising development that changed my life forever.

Most of these projects A&P got involved in didn't require the normal skills of lawyers, but rather project development experience. After getting to know me and seeing what I had done, they were convinced it was time to organize and start an affiliate of the law firm and that I should run it! This was a big surprise to me, as I was very happy in my role at Close Up and certainly wasn't looking to move on.

But after months of turning this down, I decided, with the support of my family, to try it and test my ability to convert the skills I had developed at Close Up into something new and different—and commercial. I still find it hard to understand how all this happened, but it did. I guess sometimes people see things in you that you don't see for yourself. However, I was already thirty-eight years old and, at Close Up, had the coveted corner office and a large staff. It was not easy to walk away and go to an affiliate of a law firm with a small office and half-time secretary to start. It was a big adjustment.

I have to admit that walking into a room of senior partners at A&P—many of whom had law degrees from Ivy League schools—and being questioned by them made me feel insecure. It was a real crisis of confidence. Here I was, often the only woman in the room, with these highly educated, high-powered men, and I was the daughter of immigrants who had gone to a school that housed K–12 in one building. *And* I didn't even finish high school before going to college!

In the middle of this transition and the ensuing self-questioning, I was helping my then sixteen-year-old son with his homework. For some reason, we were talking about Eleanor Roosevelt, and we came across a paragraph that served as a guidepost for the next thirty-four years. It was simple, but it was a revelation. She said, "No one can make you feel inferior without your own consent."

That was the last day of my self-doubt. I realized this was not about anyone else judging me, but rather about me judging myself. Any of the doubts I feel are my fault, no one else's. I try to remember this when I am feeling low or someone has put me down. It's not about them; it's about me. Confidence comes from within.

I came to work the next day and never looked back. Or at least almost never looked back. In those moments of weakness and self-doubt we all feel from time to time, I kept Roosevelt's little phrase tucked into my brain, and it was great medicine.

The next big career milestone for me was the breakaway of APCO from A&P and the birth of my independent company. The true story about the breakaway doesn't exist anywhere.

APCO was established as a consulting affiliate of the firm in 1984 and was the idea of a group of its partners, led by Mike Curzan, who later passed away. These partners often got together to work on projects that related to their clients but brought in both strategic and creative aspects of projects—I guess early stages of design thinking—that went far beyond what law firms do. Creating a consulting affiliate would enable these projects by collecting talented non-legal professionals in one place, representing a broad skill set.

When I finally accepted the job and got to the law firm, I learned a lot of things. For one, there was no real business plan for the operation, and some of the more traditional partners were not thrilled with the idea of having a consulting affiliate led by non-lawyers. So there was always a crosscurrent in the firm about the traditionalists who thought this was outside the scope of a first-class law firm and, therefore, either shouldn't exist or should make good money for the firm as a separate entity. Then there were the supporters of APCO who felt it could benefit their clients in a variety of ways. I reported to the policy committee of the law firm, which contained representatives of both groups.

Threading this needle and building a business was very difficult. I learned a lot during those formative years of the firm, but it definitely slowed the progression of growth. This obviously was not the core business of the law firm, and it became obvious over time that, while successful as more of a practice group, APCO would not see its full potential unless it had some freedom and ability to invest in its future. A&P professionals were critical in the process of forming APCO's DNA—high quality, ethics, standards, substantive depth—all the things that were embedded in the firm. But creativity, vision for the future, and the ability to be nimble were never going to come from being an affiliate of the law firm. That is what led to the spin-off.

At that time, APCO was working with one of A&P's partners to help a client find a PR firm for a project. In the course of running the process, I met and became interested in the firm that won the bid, GCI, which was a wholly owned affiliate of Grey Global Group, a large public holding company, and was introduced to its chairman, Ed Meyer. Ed became interested in APCO and wanted to buy the firm, or at least have me join Grey. It seemed like this global firm, which was used to having many subsidiaries, was a better place for APCO to thrive for the future, and I convinced A&P to spin us off. I made sure they received compensation for their part in starting APCO, and we maintained a good relationship post divestment. To this day, some of our best advocates are A&P partners or former partners and associates, some of whom have remained lifelong friends.

From this experience, I learned the value of relationships and fair treatment; it has always been a part of the value system at APCO. Trust, integrity, and trying to do right by people are important to me, and I think this transaction defined certain business principles that I tried to reinforce throughout the history of the firm. It was the main reason I later did a management buyout rather than selling the firm and taking the money out. I wanted to make sure that others who had helped build the firm could walk away with something more than a good reference on their resume. Having the ability to provide equity to those who helped build the firm was a really important thing to me as time went on.

Unfortunately, I have not always found partners—internally and externally—on this journey who believed in the same values, which is also a life lesson. As I have gotten older, I have placed even more value on working with and finding people who believe in the same values and see

APCO as more than a transactional place where they can extract advantage for themselves.

Dealing with the buyout and financing of the company over the years were the biggest challenges I've faced in my long career. I can't really go into detail on either this transaction or the one that eventually bought out the private equity holders that came into the firm at this time, but suffice it to say that these events caused some of my darkest moments in my career. Perhaps it is a women's issue when people with some power over your future treat you with such disrespect, but it happens—not just to me, but to many other women, as I have learned over time. It is very hard when, intellectually, you know, to some, this is a game and a way of trying to get their way or obtain some financial benefit. It is challenging when you work so hard to build something that you think is pretty special to then have to put up with and be subject to such condescending and prejudicial behaviors.

I did learn a lot in the process. I learned there are times you really need to dig deep, especially when others are counting on you. I also learned that there is real power in being underestimated. I have shared this story with other women who have experienced the same aggressive and condescending behavior. There are times it pays to bite your tongue, put your head down, and plow your way through.

Nothing proved this more than the management buyout from Grey. When Grey decided it would enable APCO to spin off, they hired an investment bank to run the process. I indicated from the outset that I wanted to do a management buyout, and they could barely contain their laughter. They would never discuss it with me and carried on with their process. I knew the deal could not happen without me, so while it was very difficult to keep quiet and not push back at their behavior, I held my fire.

When the process was finished and all the bids were in, they called to tell me what I was going to do, who was going to own APCO, and who I would work for. I had only a few words in answer: "I don't think so." These players were so arrogant that they had not read my contract, written in the early days of APCO, which declared that I had approval over anyone who would buy Grey's shares. Needless to say, their plans were never executed. They were fired for a failed process, and I worked with Grey to execute the buyout.

More than anything, these experiences are what has kept APCO independent.

When we spun off from Grey in 2004, we did it largely because Grey was about to be sold and Ed Meyer was looking toward his retirement and monetizing his sizable interest in Grey. I felt that this was the one and only time we might have to fulfill the idea of majority employee control. It was complicated, but as I said above, I was able to organize a management buyout in 2004, which has led to today's firmly independent APCO.

And yes, there have been many along the way interested in the firm's assets, but for their own benefit. No one yet has convinced me that they are interested in APCO as a legacy organization with its own value system and where first and foremost is the interest of the clients and the staff, not just the investors. I say this with all due respect to investors, as I am the largest! But I have always felt that there are three legs on the APCO stool, and all three are necessary for a stable organization:

Happy Clients: They are why we are in business—to solve their problems or create their opportunities.

Fulfilled Staff: If you cannot provide a place for people to grow and build careers and to be fulfilled at work, you will not have happy clients. Of course, this gets tricky from time to time, as some people equate fulfillment with monetary return. While I think staff should be fairly rewarded in both short- and long-term benefits, it is a balance between being fair and being responsible for the well-being of the firm.

Profitable Company: Neither of the two things above can happen if the firm is not stable, does not have money to invest in its future, cannot pay people fairly, and cannot provide a good return to its investors, who hopefully share a view on the long-term direction and investment strategy of the firm.

In a way, that is a life lesson for family as well, although the terms may differ. I think creating a family environment where there is a common view of happiness gives kids a sense of self-worth, sets mutual expectations, and establishes an understanding of the balance of personal wants and needs with those of the rest of the family's priorities, yielding fulfilled children who have stability and a good start in life.

Life is a balance of a lot of things, and so is a business. When things get out of whack, they don't work. When expectations are unreasonable, they impact the entire ecosystem, whether family or work. And underlying it all has to be a set of values that are shared. The biggest difference is that when someone is misaligned in business, there is recourse. You don't fire family!

Perhaps when I started my own business within A&P, I got my professional "wings." I never thought about where founding my own business would take me. I just wanted to offer a service that I was passionate about and thought was lacking in the marketplace. I aimed to work with and learn from people I liked and respected and believed this new platform was a place where I could make a difference in the world.

As I look back, I know there were plenty of people who thought I was crazy; others thought it was a bold move. There were many times when it was just myself in borrowed office space with a part-time secretary that thought I was crazy too.

I certainly wouldn't have guessed that APCO Worldwide would grow from one office in Washington, DC, to nearly thirty offices in twenty countries, doing business in more than eighty markets around the world. Being global— or "glocal" as I like to say—is one of the strong roots of our company. We were ahead of many trends—opening an office in Moscow in 1988, hiring an Internet guru back in 1995, establishing a presence in China well before others, and executing a management buyout when other agencies were selling their firms to major holding companies. I believe my professional "roots" helped me found the company while my "wings" kept driving me to be bold and take risks.

I am proud that my firm has been able to help our clients understand the complex and converging worlds of business, media, and public policy. We work on some of the most sensitive and important issues of our time, and we have a rigorous process for taking on new clients and their concerns. My "roots" continue to influence my actions to this day, as my firm has taken on some things that have made a real difference in people's lives, like protecting vaccine programs for kids or working with women in Africa on economic empowerment.

We have provided counsel for heads of state, wealthy business people, and lots of companies. We have always tried to do the right thing and walked away from work we feel is not appropriate or ethical. Given the nature of our business, that does not mean we avoid controversy, and sometimes others question our motives. As someone who cares deeply, it hurts when people judge you without knowing you or how deeply you feel about what you think is right. But one advantage of believing in your core values is that you have a strong guidepost that pilots you.

My son, Evan, and my daughter, Mara, work with me in the business. They both had other jobs and successful careers before they decided to join me in APCO. This was their choice, and the journey to APCO was very different for each of them. I feel very lucky to have had this professional experience with two of my kids. It adds another dimension to our relationship, and I give them a lot of credit for having the maturity to separate our family roles from our professional ones. There is something very special about sharing your passions with your kids in this intimate way.

My oldest, Lisa, whom you have already heard a lot about, does not work in the business and is a very successful television director, producer, and writer. She did a lot of freelance work in her career so she could spend time with her three kids, including homeschooling them—a commitment I am not sure I could have ever made. Besides, my kids were always so much smarter than I was! But Lisa put her same dedication into this endeavor as anyone would put into a more traditional career. At the end of the day, she made different choices than I did, and I am very proud of her ability to find her own path to success and fulfillment. As I said at the beginning of this book, each person has to take their own life's journey, and I am happy that my children had the wings to choose their own path to independence.

As Lisa has put it:

"I was on the fast track at ESPN, and I quit in 1997 for a lot of reasons. Nina, my first child, was born in 1999, and I was freelance from there. My dad thought I was crazy! My mom is amazing, but we are

different. I went to the other extreme and was stubborn, as I didn't want babysitters for my kids. This meant we had to make financial sacrifices, but it was the right choice for our family.

"You can always be replaced at the office, but you can't be replaced with your kids. Recently, I was working a Patriots/Jets game, and I could tell it affected my kids when I wasn't there. There is no substitute for a mother.

"My husband, who is an announcer for Boston Bruins (hockey) games, and I decided to arrange our lives around our kids, which included homeschooling them. We've done our best to teach them to be the best they can be, have manners, know how to meet and treat people, say thank you . . . We are so proud of them.

"I feel like I am the queen of multitasking; I can handle a lot of things at once."

I often reflect on how different my three children are and how I have learned something unique from each of them. It's important to build on and value the strengths of each individual and understand that we are all different.

Motherhood has made me a better employer and more empathetic to the needs of our staff at different stages of their careers because I get to see the impact of balancing professional life and personal obligations every day in working with and watching my own kids go through this dance.

I also believe I have learned to value the uniqueness of our employees as individuals.

Having two of my children working with me is another work and family convergence, but it certainly wasn't anything I thought would happen when I founded the company. It's been a fantastic bonus, as it's been wonderful to work with my children in interests we share. And it is quite an experience when you realize how much you learn from them.

Here's what Mara had to say:

> "I was in another career before APCO and doing well before I decided to join my mother at APCO. I had gone back to school for my MBA and wanted to do something more substantive when I finished, to put my new degree to use in my job. Before I joined APCO, I ran citywide conventions for Baltimore and, as part of that, met with a lot of people in all walks of life—local businesses, community leaders, and officials of industry associations and businesses coming to town for events. While I enjoyed it, many friends and colleagues asked me why I didn't work at my mom's company.

> "At the same time I was looking for a new opportunity, the whole extended family was together on vacation in Mexico, so my mom and I started to talk about it. Not long after the trip, I joined the company.

> "I don't need as much time as others with my mother, as I don't need a full explanation on tasks and ini-

tiatives because I know her instincts. I am proud that my efforts in marketing the firm have built her brand as well as APCO's. I am also proud that our company does things for society, to make the world better—that's a big part of why I stay.

"I enjoy my job. People think that my mother and I work more closely together than we really do. She travels so much that if I haven't seen her in a month, I'll pop my head in. Even before I joined APCO, I always worked hard. Perhaps I work harder and try to be better than everyone else to prove I deserve it.

"Margery's a role model as a mom too. Since she always worked, my brother and sister and I took turns cooking dinner and helped with our grandparents. Now, with my encouragement, my ten-year-old son learned to cook; he started with making lasagna. I hope this spirit of helping take care of family—and others—is passed down to my kids to the point that they don't have to think about it; it's just innate like it was for us growing up."

So, for me, when I talk about blending work and family, it is literally true, just as it was for my brothers and me when we worked in my father's department store. My two children who work with me understand the business challenges we face, and we confront them together, which is a gift. And we are especially careful when we are together as a family to check as much of the work at the door as possible, remembering that there are two others—my oldest daughter and my husband—who are not immersed in APCO on a daily basis. But at those times, there are usually nine grandchildren running around, so who has time to talk about work?

As a mother, I understand that tradeoffs have to be made between work and family time, and that's why our employees have the appropriate flexibility in their jobs to make it work. We try very hard at APCO to give staff durable roots by establishing our culture with a strong set of values, clear goals, and an inspiring mission. And as leaders, we have to be authentic and walk the talk so employees believe that we exemplify the values every day, with an unrelenting focus on our goals and mission.

Our employees understand that with the flexibility comes responsibility; they have to get the job done. I was pleased to hear this from one of our team members, Brent Crane, a talented and hardworking young man:

> "I am a case in point in that I am allowed to shift my schedule, get my kids from school, take them to their activities, and essentially be a full-time dad from 4:00–9:00 p.m. Then it's back on the computer to make sure things are taken care of for the next day. Of course, I am available by mobile at all times, but this has really worked for my family. I have Margery to thank for the culture and example she has set."

To help employees get their "wings," organizations must have a culture that promotes continual learning and curiosity with plenty of opportunities to grow and develop. I was determined to make this happen from very early in our company's history.

I've mentioned that being global is at our core, so as soon as we could do it, APCO offered an international exchange program. We had people go from the US to live and work in other countries and had people from other parts of the world come to the US. The problem was we didn't have the money in our early days for such a program, so our team actually hosted staff in their own homes so their colleagues could live, work, and learn in another country.

We still have a program like that today, but we don't ask the participants to stay with their colleagues!

These types of experiences are life-altering and help staff develop a global mindset. Experience like this is impressive when represented on a resume. So in this way, we give staff the opportunity to get their "wings" to expand and add to their talent tool kit. As leaders, we guide them every step of the way, rewarding them for achievement and offering advice and corrective action when mistakes are made.

I hope you can see the parallels in the ways we encourage learning with our kids and in the workplace. I'm not trying to suggest that our employees are like our children or vice versa, far from it. But there are many similarities in helping kids grow, learn, and become independent and establishing a workplace culture and environment that enables staff to develop to their fullest potential. I have learned over the years, however, not to take this concept too public because it gives off the wrong message. The analogy stops when people don't perform. Obviously, you can't fire your family at home, but at work, performance and commitment trump everything else.

I have taken great pride in seeing my children and staff use their strong roots to develop their wings. Yes, it's been tough to see them fall but so encouraging to see them get up, get back out there, and achieve great things.

Margery's Uncle Sammy (center), his brother, David (left), and a friend not long before Sammy's bone cancer was discovered. He died at twenty-one years old in 1961 and was Margery's first hero and an inspiration to her throughout her life.

Margery at a Close Up Foundation breakfast with former Congressman Bill Frenzel (R-MN) during his early years in Congress in the 1970s. Margery and Congressman Frenzel remained friends until his death in 2014.

Margery signing papers for the management buyout of APCO on
September 27, 2004, in New York City.

CHAPTER TWO

Lesson Two:
Praise in Public, Criticize in Private

"In the more than twenty years I worked with Margery, I have never witnessed an outburst, seen her express strong displeasure. She really does handle issues behind closed doors. I can guarantee that there have been many challenging days, but she handles confrontation directly, one-on-one. She doesn't beat around the bush. She knows that the team takes on the personality of the leader, and too much raving and public criticism is not her style; she doesn't demonstrate that type of behavior. She chooses to set the tone and be a role model that we can all look up to."

—LONGTIME APCO STAFF MEMBER

AS parents and as leaders at work, one of our most important jobs is building character and self-esteem. Public criticism and attacks are the fastest ways to tear people down and destroy self-confidence.

One of the guiding principles in raising my children and developing people at work has been to help them grow and learn by teaching them to deal with and overcome their mistakes. I have made it a practice to *never* publicly humiliate others. When mistakes are made, pull aside the involved individuals and have a discussion so you can help them learn and move forward in a positive way. Do not criticize in public and embarrass those who have erred.

This lesson was reinforced when I was a target of bad behavior. In the early days of APCO, when it was part of the law firm Arnold & Porter, the senior partner in charge was fiercely critical of me in front of staff. Afterward, I asked to talk to him behind closed doors. When we were alone, I told him that what he just did undermined him and his authority. He brought shame on himself, not me.

I also told him that he would never do that to me again in public. I made it clear that I was perfectly prepared to hear any criticism he had of me, but not in the hallway, at the top of his lungs, for all the staff to hear.

This particular individual was a bully, and it was important for me to set the stage with him early for how we would operate in the future. I communicated calmly and wasn't disrespectful to him in any way, as I did not want him to perceive me as a threat. Interestingly, as I had predicted, the staff lost respect for him, not me, for his behavior and comments. I made it clear that criticism should be constructive and given in private, not in a public setting. Those who witnessed his bad behavior learned from the example I set in handling it behind closed doors.

I have run across a number of bullies during my long career, and I've found it important to lay down the ground rules and call out this type of behavior as soon as it happens. It's interesting that a fairly high percentage of bullies can dish it out but can't take it. When confronted privately on their behavior, many bullies immediately back down, as they aren't used to people calling them out on how they treat others. And believe me, their bad habits will continue until they are directly asked to stop.

I have been happy to hear and be part of the national discussion on "Me Too," and while I think we need to be careful we don't take this too far out of proportion, some men have felt they had a license to abuse women over whom they had power. I don't know too many women of my age who have not had a "Me Too" moment, or moments, and they are very disempowering. At the same time, we have to support all those men who have supported us. I have been lucky to have a lot of men in my life who have helped me when I was down, provided constructive feedback when it was needed, and made me feel normal again when I had been badly bruised by destructive behavior. I worry about the lack of civility today and balancing the lesson of this chapter against today's norms of society, including the impact of social media.

It has been rather shocking to me to witness the changes in what is considered to be permissible. As Lisa said, she tried to teach her kids, as I did mine, to have manners, respect each other, and be positive contributors. I know that in Evan's and Mara's households, mutual respect is the core value, and failure to observe that has consequences. And to me, it is a core founding principle of

APCO. Yet it is hard to reinforce the importance of these values when we have given everyone a megaphone through today's politics and social media and there aren't any guidelines. When you see bad behavior, speak up; don't let it go on. Constructive criticism delivered respectfully most likely will benefit you and those around you, as they are also suffering because of the bad behavior.

My advice: both at home and in the workplace, build character and self-esteem, stand up for what is right, and treat all people with respect. We want our kids, as well as those who work for and with us, to be confident and feel good about themselves. As parents and leaders within our families and companies, we must build an environment of respect, which means never demeaning people in public. In this way, we must ask ourselves as leaders: *How do I act in public?*

If we exhibit bad behavior at work and at home, I am afraid we are setting a bad example, and our kids and those we lead could be on a track to disappoint, as they very well may follow this less-than-desirable lead.

The common threads in praising and criticizing children and staff are honesty, consistency, and respect.

I don't need to say much about honesty because, as parents and workplace leaders know, children and employees can sniff a false note from a mile away. They want—and demand—authentic parents and leaders. We must be consistent in our behavior so kids and staff know what to expect. And respect is key and a two-way street.

Praising our kids is easy to do and a pleasure. How rewarding it is when our children do the right thing, help others, say something insightful, get a great grade, make the team, graduate . . . As parents, we feel so proud. When the praise is bestowed in front of others, our children feel great pride and a real sense of accomplishment. There were so many times over the years that tears came to my eyes when my kids did something wonderful. I have to admit that it still happens, even though my oldest has just passed fifty! And now it happens with my grandkids too. The only advice here is to make sure that the praise is earned.

Too much praise, especially unearned, won't be heard over time.

A very insightful young woman once said how painful it was to her when she and her siblings were young and their mother disciplined them in public, screaming at them. It was embarrassing and humiliating, and she never forgot the feeling. The pain of it still showed on her face when she told the story years later. Obviously, this is different for very young children who need to understand cause and effect and might require more immediate action, but even in early years, there is a way to deliver your displeasure so that you can correct behavior and still build self-esteem.

The same feelings surface when someone is criticized publicly at work for others to hear. The targeted staff member ends up with a sinking feeling in his or her gut, and the co-workers look away, feeling the hurt and embarrassment of the employee receiving the criticism. It's uncomfortable for all. When employees are repeatedly dressed down in public by their leaders, the workplace becomes toxic, unproductive, and costly because good people won't stay in an environment like that. When it continually happens, good people leave.

Having said that, it's much easier *knowing* the right thing to do than actually *doing* it. Constructive criticism is an art and a science and challenging for both parties—parent and child or boss and employee. It is especially hard when you are really angry about the behavior.

Let's face it. Criticism of staff—or our kids—is hard. It's difficult to do well, as there are so many feelings involved. No one likes to be criticized, and few people get enjoyment in telling others things they don't want to hear. And when your kids disappoint, well, it can get emotional, which can cause situations to spin out of control. If not done properly, workplace criticism can do considerable damage as well.

I really believe that when it comes to doling out criticism and punishment, an old adage holds true: Treat others as you would like to be treated. This applies at home and at work.

Lots of people ask me and my children, Evan and Mara, what it's like to work together.

Here is what Evan had to say:

"As a professional colleague, she is an extraordinary practitioner in our field. Related or not, the business she built is impressive, and she has an incredible way of working and an ability to do great things. She excels.

"When she is in a brainstorm session or involved with the clients, the work is just better. As an employee, you want to be in a place that feels like, at end of day, you are treated fairly and trusted. I know that my mother has my best interests in mind, which frees me up to do what's best for the company and clients.

"We don't always agree, as we have different views and are not of one mind, and when we do have big disagreements, neither one of us questions the other's intention. Of course, strong disagreements are hard for me, hard for her. Who am I to tell her what should be?

"As it's a family company, there is always a little twinge that hurts my credibility, and that is a challenging aspect for me. But there's more good than bad. Otherwise, I wouldn't be here."

I have professional and personal relationships with my two children that I work with, and it's important to keep the different relationships separate as much as possible. Sometimes this is especially difficult when you know your children, in their professional capacity, are accomplishing great things, but you cannot praise them too much for it. I find that hard because they make a big difference in their jobs, and if they were not my kids, I would be saying a lot more about their performance in a public way. Perhaps this mention will let them know how much they are appreciated and how valuable their support and input have been to me.

I know my son, Evan, who is such an accomplished executive in the company, will not be pleased that I tell this story, as this incident happened a long time ago when he was a teenager, but it is a good illustration of the lesson of this chapter: praise in public, criticize in private.

His behavior at the time surprised and shocked us. Needless to say, he disappointed his father and me and was punished.

When Evan was seventeen, he took the car and went out with his friends. Later in the evening, after being at a house party with a group of friends, he was ready to leave and gave his car keys to his friend, as he knew he had drunk too much to drive. He went out to the car, which was parked in front of this house, to try to sober up, and he proceeded to throw up all over the car. Sensing commotion and trouble right outside of their house, the neighbors called the police. As he wasn't driving, Evan wasn't charged, but the incident scared him—and us—to death.

Here's what we did. We waited until he was totally sober the next morning and talked to him privately about his behavior and what he needed to do to redeem himself. He was already embarrassed enough about what had happened; he didn't need his parents to yell at him in front of his siblings.

Of course, Steve and I were gratified that he had chosen not to drive and handed over the keys. This was a smart thing to do, and we told him so. We discussed the responsibility of driving and that drinking and getting behind the wheel was not a combination that was safe for him or others and he should never do it. Perhaps drinking that much was something that a lot of young people do on a dare, but we made it clear this was unhealthy and unacceptable.

He apologized for his behavior, which we appreciated. However, he needed to make it up to others as well, so instead of grounding him, we told him he must go and apologize to the neighbors and the police for his behavior. Visiting the neighbors and the police station to say he was sorry was not easy, but he did it. We criticized him in private and insisted that he make amends on his own and quite publicly. It was a lesson learned for life. So even out of adversity, parents can feel proud of their children!

Evan's View:

"While I'm not saying it's the right thing to do, a night of drinking is a rite of passage for lots of teenagers. Most people attempt to have a healthy relationship with alcohol rather than a destructive one. It's unfortunate that my first opportunity consuming hard alcohol was awful. I wasn't used to it, and I drank more than I should without knowing. I felt sick and embarrassed about what happened. The police called my parents and said, 'Come and pick up what is left of your son.'

"I didn't feel very well that evening or the next morning, but I remember the lesson: face up to your mistakes. My parents told me that what I did was wrong but that it wasn't in my character to act that way

and I had to make up for my mistake. It was embarrassing. Dealing with the ramifications was equally embarrassing.

"It's interesting that this experience helped me deal with an incident recently with my teenage daughter and alcohol. We had a real conversation about drinking, thanks to what happened to me and the way my parents dealt with me so many years ago."

All people, children or adults, are different, and praise and criticism must be delivered in a way that works best for each individual and situation. Let me explain. I've had staff members who responded more to a "kick in the pants" type of criticism and others who needed a much lighter touch. You've got to figure out the personality type you are dealing with and the best way to deliver criticism for that person.

A lighter touch would never work with the "kick in the pants" guy I worked with, as the words would just roll off of him. With this particular individual, I needed to be clear and to the point when he screwed up, even displaying some anger so he understood the gravity of the situation. He generally realized when he had made a mistake or misjudged a situation, so I was pretty much telling him something he already knew. With this staff member, I would be clear on what he needed to do to correct the situation, whom he needed to address, and the timeframe in which he had to do it. He understood, acknowledged his error, and left my office with clear direction.

Just as the light touch doesn't work for some on the team, the "kick in the pants" approach could devastate another staff member. I worked with a very talented individual who just needed what I'd call "gentle coaching" to stay on track. As a leader, make sure you understand which approach is going to help the individual correct the mistake and move past it effectively, hopefully learning a lesson along the way. In all cases, keep your criticism private and your praise as public as appropriate.

Delivering consistently effective constructive criticism to help staff grow and develop in the workplace is one of the most difficult challenges for a leader.

It's interesting that the head of a baseball team is not called a coach, but a manager. Baseball may seem like the easiest game in the world to play: throw the ball, catch the ball, hit the ball. However, it is almost entirely the way you manage people and personalities against your strategy that builds and maintains a successful team.

Another tip: As a leader, always give credit for success to others. Never take it for yourself. That holds true for parenting, too, as you should give all the credit to your kids when they do something wonderful. All you need to do is stand back and bask in their achievements. And I do.

(Left to right) Evan, Lisa, Steve, Margery, and Mara Kraus.
For Margery and Steve's 25th anniversary in 1991, their kids
arranged a surprise party at a park near their home in Virginia.

Margery at a women's leadership conference in Abu Dhabi in 2014,
sponsored by the United Arab Emirates Government.

CHAPTER THREE

_____

Lesson Three:
Be Fearless

I often think of the quote from President John F. Kennedy when he made his inspiring speech about the US program to land a man on the moon, and I'll paraphrase here: We don't do these things because they are easy. We do them because they are hard.

It isn't easy to achieve your dreams; it takes commitment and hard work, along with the courage to take risks.

I truly believe that being fearless starts early—back to roots and wings again—so I must go back in time to pinpoint moments of courage from my past. It might be a great exercise for you to think about the times you were fearless while facing challenges.

I do think that one must have confidence to be fearless.

I started developing professional confidence when I worked at my dad's store, and I believe that helped me when I started working with the football team. I have to laugh when I think of myself—a girl, a teenager—dealing confidently with these athletic men from all different backgrounds and working my way through some pretty dicey situations.

Confidence, plus a sense of curiosity about the world—about different cultures and people who are different—certainly fed my desire to be fearless.

When I was sixteen, an Austrian neurologist, whom my family and I met when he did a rotation in the US, asked me to be his family's au pair in Austria for the summer. We got to know this doctor while he was treating my Uncle Sammy during the last six months of his life as he struggled with his cancer.

Of course I agreed to go to Austria! I never thought anything about traveling on my own and living in a country where I did not speak the language. I was excited about the challenge of it all and confident in my ability to navigate and thrive in a new country.

As soon as I arrived, I started to teach the kids English, and they taught me German. On my way there and on my way home, as well as on the few days I had off, I traveled around Europe, seeing amazing sights I had only read about, reveling in the adventure of it all. I met so many interesting people, particularly on trains. They would invite me to their homes, and I went! Remember, this was more than fifty years ago. How wonderful it was to be welcomed into someone's home, taste home-cooked meals of local delicacies, and learn about a different culture and country than my own. I wasn't naive and chose carefully, but I wouldn't trade these experiences for the world. I loved drinking everything in—the wonderful sights, the warm and welcoming people. I guess I was fearless, but I learned so much, including about myself.

Not long after I returned, I made up my mind to go to college early (at the end of my junior year) and, as I said before, went to college before I graduated from high school. I convinced three schools that I was ready for admission, and they agreed, although this was not the normal process! It helped that I had taken almost all the senior courses in my school and both my grades and test scores were acceptable. After this incredible experience of being on my own in Europe, I convinced these admissions officers that it was hard to come back to my high school (kindergarten through twelfth grade in one building) and feel challenged. Next, I convinced my parents that if I could get accepted to three colleges after my junior year, they should let me go. After all, if three schools put me through their admissions process and agreed that I was ready for college, I must be ready!

I applied and ended up going to Knox College in Galesburg, Illinois, where my older brother was enrolled and where my father went before he left college for World War II.

Perhaps in hindsight, I should have finished high school first, but I took a chance and went to college—and it didn't faze me. I actually didn't graduate from high school until well after I finished college and my master's degree. I guess I've never really followed the rules very well! The only person truly upset about this is my oldest daughter, who was a junior in high school when I received my honorary high school degree. She was mad that I didn't wait another year so we could be in the same graduating class—at least by year.

Sadly, my high school does not exist anymore. The

building is now only an elementary school, and kids from my hometown go to a regional high school, where I am sure there is a lot more diversity in the curriculum. Still, there was something special about being in one class with the same kids for all those years. In fact, we still have all-class reunions, and I love to go and catch up with these friends of more than sixty years. One proud moment for me was to be able to include my school in Close Up, which was special for all of them. In return, the school awarded me with the last diploma from the high school, which is how I received my high school diploma years after getting my master's degree.

I remember one of the toughest times in my life that courage and being fearless helped get me through—my parents' divorce. I know there was a time when my parents were really in love. They were a beautiful couple. My mother was stunning and my dad a real ladies' man. Although they were both born in Poland, their paths to the US were very different. My dad came as a young child and never knew another life than the one here. He was very American—no accent, a real sports fan, and, except for the war, not widely traveled.

My mother went from Poland to Cuba and grew up there and was much more Cuban in her formative years than either Polish or American. It sometimes was part of her charm. Her family was very close and often spoke only in Spanish, although they were all able to speak English. They were just more comfortable speaking Spanish when they were all together, which is very common in immigrant families. I grew up learning kitchen Spanish—the Spanish you learn working with the women of the family in the kitchen. While I didn't realize it at the time, I think it made me very comfortable around a broad variety of people.

My parents were both good parents—but different. They each influenced me in different ways. They were decent people with good values and generous to strangers. We were not affluent, but in our small town, we were solidly middle class. Memories of childhood were shaped by living in a small town where everyone knew each other, and my family was very well known because of our store. Certain behaviors were expected. We had a lot of independence but a lot of responsibility, which is probably the best lesson of all. Those two things are linked—responsibility and freedom. Perhaps this was my first attraction to roots and wings —a life philosophy that governed my own value system that I have now seen at work for my kids and my grandchildren, as well as my company.

My mother overthought everything and had difficulty making decisions. I think this was partly her inclination to defer to my dad, and part of it was her own insecurity. When I was a junior in high school, we moved into a new house. My mother built this house as her "dream," as we had lived in very tight quarters from the time I could remember. By today's standards, the house was very modest, but it was a milestone for her. Once the house was built, it was not furnished, except for what we'd brought with us. My mother simply could not make up her mind about what she wanted. So one day, my dad and I, tired of living without some of the basics (couch in the family room, for instance), went out and bought several rooms full of furniture! I think my mother was more relieved than upset.

My dad and I were very close. We both were very spontaneous. We would get an idea and move on it. Sometimes that impulsiveness was fun. Sometimes it was irresponsible. On the fun side, my dad, my brothers, and I were once on our way to the airport to go to Miami, Florida, where my mother was already on vacation. When we got to Newark's airport, it was snowing hard, and the airport was closed. My dad never stopped. We all got in the car and drove without a second thought!

Sometimes his impulsiveness had really significant consequences, and it ultimately led to my parents' separation.

From the time I understood enough about life, I knew that my father cheated on my mother. It was a small town, after all. I could see the heartache that eventually caused them to grow further and further apart. It made my mother ill, or perhaps exacerbated a mental illness she already had that was later diagnosed. This tough time in their relationship, which ultimately led to my father running off with his high school girlfriend (they later married), was hardest on my younger brother, who was in high school at the time. I was already in college and on a path that led me to marry Steve.

The divorce, like so many, was painful for the family. My mother grew up in a situation where family life was the most important thing. My dad, not so much. His family had splintered in a lot of ways.

My dad was already committed to moving on and my mom to holding on. She was also concerned about her future. My parents sold the store. There was no nest egg of significance for my mother, and she had no background for employment. Where would she live? Staying in the small town was not really an option for her. (She ultimately moved to Queens, New York, and then to Florida, in both cases to be near family. Part of that transition time also had her living with me and my family, especially when she needed medical help.)

Since they were not agreeing on divorce terms and my dad was already with someone else, I decided the best thing I could do was sit down with them both and get them to settle. I prompted my father to commit to terms that he would keep and that would take some of the insecurity out of my mother's life. Because my dad and I were close, I got him to promise certain basic things to my mother—a promise he kept for the rest of her life.

I was only twenty-one when this was going on, but I was already married and just had a child. Taking on the responsibility for my parents, especially my mother, and worrying about my younger brother definitely impacted my idea of family. And being married to Steve while going through this, I am sure, reinforced our commitment to having a different kind of family life, especially since his family was totally dissimilar.

Evelyn and Ben Kraus were ten years older than my parents and deeply devoted to each other. In Steve's family, his grandmother, who lived only a few blocks from his family home in Brooklyn, made breakfast every Sunday in their small apartment for all the kids, spouses, and grandchildren. You did not decline. I met the Kraus family when I'd just turned seventeen and started dating Steve. I was immediately embraced into this tight-knit unit (except for Taffy, Steve's dog, who was always jealous). I was lucky to have this anchor while going through such turmoil in my own family. Given that this is an important part of Steve's upbringing, it is easy to understand how family came to dominate our own thinking about life's values.

After my father married Nicki, his high school sweetheart, we were kept at a distance, even though we were kind to her. It was only after Nicki passed away and he moved in with us that my dad learned the names of my grandchildren! He lived with us for almost three years, and he died at ninety-three. We all treasured that time with him.

Courage and fearlessness are important professionally too. Early in my career, I decided I had to be fearless. At the Close Up Foundation, we scheduled lots of well-known speakers so the students could learn from them. When I had the assignment of booking prominent people, I remember staring at the phone, trying to figure out how to approach famous, powerful people to ask them to speak at our small nonprofit. Well, it didn't take me long to figure out that I just needed to pick up the phone and call, so I did.

It was a different time in Washington (early 70s), and I came up with some strategies to get the potential speakers on the phone. To try and get a Supreme Court justice,

I figured out if I called after five in the evening, I might just get someone who wasn't used to screening calls. It probably wasn't proper, but what did I know? I was twenty-three years old and had a job to do! And it worked.

One day, Tom Clark, Associate Justice of the Supreme Court of the United States from 1949 to 1967, did answer the phone and, even more amazingly, agreed to speak at our event. Over time, as Justice Clark became a friend and supporter of the program, he helped me learn about the inner workings of the court and get to know about half of the Supreme Court justices at that time. That led to a treasure trove of experiences and opportunities both for me and Close Up.

Emboldened by my early success, I kept picking up the phone to bring in extraordinary people to speak. I was very fortunate to build relationships with a number of them. In the case of the Close Up Foundation, we had a noble mission, and many prominent figures in politics and business believed in what we were trying to accomplish in developing informed citizens, so they agreed to help us.

I also learned two important lessons. People, even those who seem unapproachable, are just people. They respond to passion and authenticity, so never be afraid to approach them. The worst thing that can happen is a turndown. I also learned that if you are afraid to ask, you will never get a positive response. "Because you asked me" is a really important reason people say yes.

No one taught me more than Hubert Humphrey Jr., the longtime senator from Minnesota, vice president, and another of my speaker targets. I much admired Humphrey and thought he would be a great speaker for our students. In trying to schedule him, I gave him thirteen dates and let him know that I thought he could turn me down once, but not thirteen times. And to my surprise, he accepted all thirteen! I once asked him why, and he told me the story about his mother meeting Harry Truman. Humphrey was a new senator and approached Truman, who ended up meeting Humphrey's mother. The impact that meeting had on Mrs. Humphrey was profound, so Hubert vowed to make himself accessible because he knew that personal contact like the kind his mother had with President Truman was incredibly important.

I would never have known that or enjoyed the personal relationship I developed with Hubert Humphrey had I been afraid to step forward. This experience repeated itself many times in my life, and I have been very fortunate in my career to enjoy scores of wonderful relationships that started with me picking up the phone or initiating a conversation when given the opportunity.

Many connections that I and others at APCO Worldwide have developed started with me going up to total strangers. Many times, I've heard an intriguing speaker and then approached him or her and asked if we could meet for coffee in DC to follow up. It all starts with one approach. If you can develop the courage—the fearlessness—to do this, it is truly amazing what you can achieve. I like to call it "calibrated persistence."

When I think about it today and the tremendous network of friends and acquaintances I have made over the years, I reflect on how a small-town girl, the child of immigrants and someone with no connections, was able to build such a network. It is a reminder that courage and initiative can often substitute for other less controllable things that come from privilege and connections.

The reason I could be persistent was that I was confident (at least on the outside!), believed in what I was doing and what I was "selling," and had the fundamental belief that people needed me and what my organization was offering. I also learned that it was important to present things in a clear way that communicated why what you were suggesting was good for the person you were trying to reach.

In terms of being fearless, sometimes you have to pick up the phone and make the first move in your career or life. You'll get plenty of rejections, so steel yourself, but, oh, when you are able to accomplish your goals, do good, and perhaps build relationships that last a lifetime, well, rewarding doesn't fully cover it. Be fearless, be confident, and don't be afraid to fail, because that is exactly how you ultimately win personally and professionally. It is also an important life lesson for your kids and their success. Of course, you have to make sure they don't equate fearlessness with acts of irresponsible action!

Margery on Capitol Hill with Hubert Humphrey, long-time senator from Minnesota and vice president from 1965–1969.

(L to R) Speaker of the House Tip O'Neill, Hal Walker of CBS, Congressman Bill Frenzel (R-MN), Margery Kraus, and Steve Janger, the President of Close Up in the late 1970s, on Capitol Hill.

CHAPTER FOUR

Lesson Four:
Nurture—Don't Underestimate the Power of Caring

CARING does start with family and your roots. I learned early on from my parents and from my experience in my father's store that if you go out of your way for people, then they will likely do the same for you. Besides, it is the right thing to do. And I have always done that in my personal and professional life.

It is also disappointing to learn that people don't always reciprocate, so this "caring" has to come from a genuine desire to do things that give you pleasure in the "doing" and not because you expect some reciprocal action. Most people are more than appreciative, but I have learned in life, there are truly some people who have a gross sense of entitlement and will disappoint. That is a good life lesson but should not deter you from doing the right thing or going out of your way to help people. Caring is a reward in itself.

At times, my husband thought I was insane, as he believed that I was making WAY too much effort for people. Through my work and at home, I would do things that would keep me up all night, but I knew the extra effort and caring was an important way for me to express my love or respect, regardless of whether or not it would be appreciated. Most of the time, I was genuinely surprised that people were so appreciative of small acts of kindness.

Let me give you a few examples.

We attended a good friend's daughter's wedding recently. One of my hobbies is photography. Those who know me well constantly see me with a camera around my neck. I love snapping photos around the world. I brought my camera to the wedding, and I was thinking about the bride and groom and how they miss so much of the wedding, as they are often hidden away from the crowds and activities. There are a million things going on that they don't see, particularly in advance of the wedding ceremony. And the photos the professionals snap take a while to get back.

So on the wedding day, I made a point to sneak around everywhere I could to take photos, some behind the scenes and others just as events unfolded in view of everyone attending. It was a wonderful wedding, and Steve and I stayed fairly late, with me continuing to take photos. When we left, I went to a twenty-four-hour pharmacy with a photo shop and got my photos printed and bought frames to feature wonderful shots of the bride and groom and their families, some more formal, some entirely behind the scenes.

The next day, we were invited to the bride's parents' house to see the newly married couple opening gifts. When I presented the framed photographs to the bride and groom in front of their stunned parents and families, well, all were overwhelmed. I wish I could express how important the moment was, both to me and to those gathered. Yes, I did lose some sleep, but the reward I got far exceeded the sacrifice. It was especially meaningful to have these photos in real time to reflect on the moment and relive the beautiful feelings all over again. I loved that it made a difference to my friend and her family.

That attitude is the same one I've brought to my working life. I remember way back, in the years when APCO was part of Arnold and Porter, there was an important client coming to town. Most thought that we would just set up a meeting with the client and that would be it. Not me. I called the client, told him I would pick him up at the airport, and invited him to dinner.

I did it because I had an interest in getting to know him better. He accepted my offer, and I actually took him to the Senate and we were able to visit the Senate Dining Room. From the time we spent together, we developed a wonderful professional relationship. I treasure those relationships that I have been able to develop over my professional life. But I did go the extra mile. I did try to nurture those relationships, perhaps more than most people would. But, again, I did it not to curry favor or win business, but because I had a real curiosity about the person and wanted to get to know more about the individual. I also wanted the individual to know that we valued him as more than a client.

Partly because of my intense focus on relationships, I put together an International Advisory Council for APCO Worldwide, which has leading experts from around the world to lend their advice and expertise to APCO and its clients. These impressive professionals range from former politicians to corporate executives to prominent civil servants. Many of the relationships I have with these folks go back more than forty years. There are times I've asked them for help and other times when they've approached me for assistance. We help each other. These relationships bring additional meaning to work and make it much more than a job.

To see someone touched by something I've done for them, something I consider such a small thing . . . well, it does make my day. Many times, I've seen a cynical individual somewhat emotional when I—or someone around me—has taken the time to care, to nurture a particular interest. It is always amazing to me how few people do these things.

Here's an example I have built into my working life. I write personal notes and sign anniversary cards for every employee on work anniversaries. That's almost eight hundred cards a year! When I go around the world, I see a lot of people have these notes of appreciation posted at their work stations. Occasionally, I get incredible notes back, especially from people who don't know me and are surprised to receive a personal note from the chairman. I have even been asked if I write these myself—which, of course, I do!

I've heard that some people have said these notes have made a difference to them. If so, I am incredibly pleased. I make a practice of doing these when I travel, as I am on the road so much. It's actually enjoyable for me to do this, adding a note on the individual's contributions to our company at the hotel following a long day at Davos, meetings with clients in the Middle East, a speech in Asia, a staff event at one of our many US offices, or a visit with a potential client in Europe.

Here are two recent notes I received after sending the cards:

"I received your wonderfully thoughtful handwritten card on the occasion of my second work anniversary here at APCO. I felt special and very happy receiving that note from you. Can't thank you enough. I have not yet had a chance to meet you in person, but I hope to meet you sometime soon. For me, it's always fascinating to hear and learn from people like you who have built reputed companies like APCO brick by brick, layer by layer over so many years. I often wonder what it takes to achieve something which needs a confluence of people, ideas, wherewithal, and energy to seamlessly come together and carve out a niche for itself under the sun."

—A two-year veteran of our team in India

"I am writing to you to say thank you [personally] for the marvelous gesture you make each year of complimenting every employee on their anniversary milestones with that handwritten card.

"While it might come through to many as a simple corporate goodwill gesture, having lived and assimilated the APCO culture over the last five

years, I realize how much this means to the morale and spirit of every employee.

"It has been a pleasure and privilege to be part of APCO Worldwide's Arab Region head office over the last five years, and I have learnt so much. I do not believe I have been so proud of any of my previous workplaces—and in 25 years as a media professional, that speaks volumes.

"And allow me to add that you continue to remain an inspiration with all you do!"

—A five-year member of our team in the Middle East

You can understand why I take this exercise so seriously! It makes a connection I can't always do on a personal basis, given the size of the company and the demands on my time.

I suppose I shouldn't be surprised that in this high-tech electronic age, relationships can be lost, but I have to admit that I don't understand why more people don't go out of their way for each other personally and professionally. It's so rewarding and makes work—and life—more fun.

I also believe these kinds of acts do rub off on others. I have seen that my children and grandchildren often take on things that give pleasure to others. Whether volunteering at the library, visiting senior citizens, or helping at their temple, they find ways to show their compassion and care for others. And they have gotten that special feeling that comes from knowing they made a difference.

There are many ways this has carried over into business. From the inception, APCO has always been involved in doing pro bono work, both as an organization or represented by individual staff members who volunteer. We have been especially engaged in projects that center around the advancement of women and their economic independence, since we are a majority woman-owned business, one of the few of scale in our industry. But our work is not limited to that.

More recently, we have developed a framework for taking on issues of importance in society where we can use our campaign skills and team up with experts in the field who have solutions that can make a difference. A good example is our work with Dr. Ron DePinho, a world-class cancer specialist who is the former head of MD Anderson.

Ron is dedicating a significant part of his time to help create a movement to help educate and encourage young adults and those that influence them to take actions now that will prevent cancers later in life. We helped to form the Unite to Prevent Cancer Foundation and create the action steps to support this massive education and action movement.

I hope we can build on this model in the future for other "change the world" issues, fully utilizing APCO's experience, contacts, and global platform.

CHAPTER FIVE

Lesson Five: No Whining

I'LL admit up front that in the last couple of years, I have violated this rule. We completed a comprehensive refinancing of APCO Worldwide and worked some complicated issues for clients during this time, and it was challenging to say the least. In the process of all of this going on and as a result of the process, I had a very sad ending to a very long friendship that hurt me to the core.

So I am sorry that I broke my own rule, but I can say with all honesty that I really do try not to complain or whine, both professionally and personally.

But I guess we all have our limits.

During all of this, I developed cancer. I was very lucky because I caught it early, and at the first sign, I went to the doctor and took care of it. It was uterine cancer in its early stages, and, at my age, that was a body part no longer necessary, so I felt very fortunate.

We all are sometimes pushed to the limits in both patience and professionalism, and it becomes easy to feel sorry for ourselves. I am no exception to that. In retrospect, I think we all have moments when it seems as though those around us have disappointed us, and we have to take extra care that we don't allow these moments to fundamentally change who we are and how we treat others.

This is especially true with "taking work home." I have always been careful not to allow the stresses of the day to influence how I behave at home. Sometimes that is really hard, but it is important that we don't draw upon our frustrations in the wrong way with the wrong people.

Here's my philosophy: Life has its ups and downs, and rather than spend our time complaining when things aren't going our way, we all have to learn to do something about it. It's really that simple.

I always told my kids, "You can spend all your time whining or spend the time getting it done." Whining doesn't make things go faster or better. Save your energy.

The truth is, at home and at work, no one wants to hear people complaining and taking the "half-empty" approach to life or their career. Who wants to be around "half-empty" people? It's no fun, as they suck the energy out of the room. I once heard a speaker do a workshop where we all did an exercise turning the things we complain about into positive things to improve. It was amazing to me to think about how much time and energy is wasted complaining and saying negative things about others. During my own lapses, the kids have had to remind me!

Perhaps it's just my glass-half-full personality, but I work hard to see the good in people and things. Sometimes, when you are in the middle of it all, it is especially hard.

In 2010, my family was hit with a wave of very difficult things to face. I had surgery on my foot, which turned out to be the least of things. My daughter-in-law, Claudette, was diagnosed with breast cancer and underwent a double mastectomy and chemo. Just when the two of us were in the midst of these health issues, my granddaughter, Leighton (the youngest of my son's four children), contracted near-fatal encephalitis. After a month in the hospital to stabilize her, Leighton—then two and now eleven—had to spend the next three months at Kennedy Krieger Center at Johns Hopkins in rehabilitation to relearn how to walk, talk, and eat.

While all this was going on, my father's wife died, and my father came to live with us. Then I lost one of my closest cousins. It was all too much. Oh yes, *and* we needed to keep the business moving forward because it was important to keep the momentum going for our teams around the world.

I know these do not sound like stories from a very optimistic person, but there was so much good that came from this experience. It just took a while to realize it. Evan never left his daughter's bedside for four months, except to see his wife and other kids while we substituted at the medical facility. Family and friends rallied. Evan and Claudette's friends were unbelievable, bringing them food so they didn't have to cook, mowing their lawn, helping with childcare. Co-workers at the office gladly jumped in to back Evan's work and held a fundraiser for the institution that was taking such good care of Leighton. Everyone got involved.

But what I learned most of all was how lucky we were. Sitting one night at Kennedy Krieger to give Evan a break, I talked to some of the other parents who were sleeping in chairs next to their kids who faced similar trauma. Hearing their stories was heartbreaking. Some had to quit their jobs to take care of their child. Others had no health insurance and had to sell off their assets to help their child learn to walk after a trauma. Some of the babies had been born addicted. Others did not live nearby and had to leave the rest of their family to take care of their sick child. And here I was with a strong family to support all of our challenges that year, good health insurance, jobs that would not be lost, and a prognosis that while recovery on all fronts would be slow and steady, it would come. I guess it is true that what doesn't kill you makes you stronger. And perhaps it takes this kind of adversity to help reset priorities and a sense of positivity.

One of the most inspiring things that came from this experience is that Evan wrote a daily blog that kept everyone up to date on the challenges and progress and his personal emotions going through all of this. It was incredibly honest, and beyond our family, perfect strangers started reading it and we were hearing from people across the country who were rooting for Leighton's and Claudette's recovery. So while 2010 was an incredibly stressful year and I would not want to repeat it for anything, in retrospect, it made me realize that some things are more important than everything else and to let go of petty issues.

All in all, I try to keep a positive spirit because I believe it is healthy and can be infectious to those in your care. I think it came from the roots I developed when I first got married.

I mentioned earlier in the book that I never thought about being a working mother and certainly not working 'round the clock. I have had to juggle lots of things, and, especially when tired, it is easy to complain or at least to find fault in others who do not seem to be holding up their part of this bargain. I did make one promise to myself that perhaps is a reflection of my generation of women who were not groomed to work. I promised myself that, especially working in the crazy jobs I have had that required much more than a forty-hour week, I would not complain. I signed up for being a wife and mother first, and I would not use my work as an excuse for giving short shrift to those important parts of my life. I would find a way to cope and not whine.

This turned out to be very important both in my personal coping and in my family life. Over time, coping meant building teamwork both at home and at the office, which has supported me in the grind of work but also with the emotional stress of living a complex life. I have had the good fortune to be surrounded by people who care and who come together when things get tough. It is often too easy to feel sorry for yourself when you are overwhelmed, so you really need to make sure that you don't default to blaming others. Just get on with it! Make lists and attack. Delegate what you can. But don't whine. Most likely, if you are anything like me, you have brought this on yourself.

I've always told my family and staff not to spend time saying negative things about people and/or situations. Instead of negative griping, turn that energy into more positive actions. It is not easy to do, and we are all guilty of breaking this rule at times. The result is that you will feel better about yourself, your world. I hate to sound Pollyanna, but I believe it's really true.

The interesting thing is if you can say one thing but do another, the lesson is lost both in the workplace and at home. You've got to "walk the talk." It's so important to teach kids early on that whining doesn't win the day. We, as parents and leaders, must set the example by not whining. I guess that's why I admitted up front that I broke my own rule, because it is so important to set the example. Shame on me for falling down on the job and not living up to my own standards.

Over time, I have worked with some of the smartest, most accomplished people who, unfortunately, shared the fatal flaw of being critical of everyone and everything, whining about their pay, their colleagues, clients . . . It's an incredible downer for everyone and literally awful to be around them. These folks were smart and could solve just about any problem, but time after time, they just couldn't get out of their own way in order to be successful. Individuals like this don't stay at a company for long, as these negative folks get found out and no one wants to work with them. The sad thing is that they impress on the way in before their true colors come out. It's challenging for those people who work with and for them.

As leaders, we do our best to work with them and counsel them, but, unfortunately, it is difficult for the vast majority of "whiners" to truly change, as the pattern was either set early in their childhood or rewarded along the way. When they see that there is no big raise or advancement for them, they often leave, going to another company, and the cycle begins again. It's not an exaggeration to say that staff are relieved to see the backs of whiners as they walk out the door.

The ability to be a constructive employee or leader may be set early. When kids whine because they want something, try to help them understand that whining doesn't help. Children should work for what they want and treat those around them with respect. If they learn early that they can whine or act out and get what they want, they may end up being one of those glass-half-empty people who complain and constantly gripe to get their way, making life miserable for those around them.

This is why I am so hard on myself for backsliding in the last few years and whining, especially after the lessons of 2010, because I know I have to set the example. It's just so important to find the good things in life, the humor, even when things seem difficult. And always focus on solutions, not problems. Yes, there are difficulties in life and work, but focus on how to overcome them. Don't wallow in them.

So to those around me who heard me whining the last few years about investors, the refinancing process, and related matters, I'm sorry and will try not to whine in the future. I am committed to making sure I focus on being the best wife, mother, grandmother, family member, friend, colleague, and leader I can be by focusing squarely on being positive and productive, even when working through challenging work and life problems.

Margery inspiring the APCO team in Shanghai in 2014.

Margery's son, Evan, with his daughter, Leighton, who was battling near-fatal encephalitis in 2010. Her mother, Claudette, was diagnosed with breast cancer and underwent a double mastectomy and chemo at the same time. Leighton, two in 2010 and now eleven, had to spend three months in rehabilitation to relearn how to walk, talk, and eat.

CHAPTER SIX

Lesson Six:
Make a Difference

THERE'S a reason my name isn't on the door of my company. I've always felt and told the staff that we are in the "we" business, not the "me" business. You don't build a professional services business without a sense of team spirit and the collective effort of a number of people. This is also what led to the management buyout in 2004 and the ability to share the equity of the firm broadly with a number of key staff. I had a chance to make a lot of money by selling the firm at that time, rather than reinvesting to build for the future, but I am really proud that the result of this choice has led to a number of my colleagues doing very well for themselves as they have exited the firm or retired.

I hope that when I am no longer a part of my firm, the legacy will be that we made a difference in the lives of individuals, as well as added great value to our clients. I am always gratified when clients say one of the reasons they like working with us is that we treat the relationship like it's more than a job. I hope that will always be the case. We should not be in business unless we really believe we can make a difference for our clients and create that fulfillment of a job well done for our staff.

Thus, no name on the door. I believe it's what we leave behind that makes a difference—what we do, not what we say or call ourselves.

I believe this desire to make a difference is something I have instilled in my family as well. It definitely is something I learned growing up. As I mentioned, my mother was raised in Cuba. After Castro came to power, the family members that remained in Cuba tried to leave and eventually were able to go, one at a time, with only the clothes on their backs. My cousin, Doranna, came when she was a teenager—about my age at the time—without her parents and to a new country where she didn't speak the language proficiently. A while later, her brother came, but it was a couple of years before her parents came. She lived with my grandmother, as did my aunt and uncle and their family when they came from Cuba. In this very personal way, I learned a lot about how important it is to share and help others in their time of need. It stuck and influenced me a lot.

I also learned these values from my parents—from my dad through the way he helped those less fortunate, providing store credit when people needed it, and from my mom through her religious beliefs.

In Judaism, there is a word, *tzedakah*, which in English is charity or giving aid, assistance, and money to the poor and needy or to worthy causes. In other religions, I have come to know that the same concept applies, like *Sadaqah* in Islam. However, the nature of these words is very different than charity. The root of the word tzedakah means righteousness, justice, or fairness. So helping others who need it is simply an act of justice, doing what is right. For me, it's living a life of meaning and trying to make a difference. I've tried to do this both personally with my family and in my private life and in passing this down to our children and grandchildren and professionally in creating the right value system in the company and in my volunteer activities.

When I volunteered my time to help others, I involved my kids from the time they were small. It was important to get them involved early so they could see that their actions to help those in need made a difference. Through their involvement in Scouts, they often took on projects to help others, whether it was food drives, volunteering to clean up playgrounds, or gathering presents and distributing them for the holidays. Giving back became a natural part of our lives, and I am pleased to see this continue in the next generations.

Once you have this drive to help others, it continues throughout life. For example, after my son's wedding, he and his bride took the flowers to senior homes, and those flowers brought joy to others. If you breed a culture of consideration for others, of giving back, it comes naturally to always think about the well-being of others, even on occasions of great joy and importance.

My daughter, Mara, is always volunteering to help. She

is the chair of the fundraising committee at her temple and a myriad of other things with her family.

Another small example from my kids' childhood: Our whole family worked to save the trees near our house, as the city and county were planning to cut them down. We involved the children in all our efforts, including research on the problem, coming up with potential solutions, and community activities that involved us speaking out. My husband testified at a public forum in front of the town council, and our kids were in the front row with shirts that read: "My Dad's the Greatest." So, again, the kids saw this spirit of activism from the time they were really little, and it grew inside of them as they became active and involved adults. If you start young, showing them action toward the greater good, they will embrace this in their lives.

This specific incident turned out to have an impact beyond our expectations. Those saved and beautiful trees now sit behind my son's house, as he bought our home when we moved out, so our grandchildren now benefit from that beauty and shade!

Our generosity and desire to help sometimes got put to the test by our kids. One day our youngest daughter, Mara, came home to tell us that she had invited a classmate to live with us!

Mara had befriended a new girl at school who was facing some incredible life challenges. She had divorced parents. Her mother didn't want her in the house because she was living with a new and younger boyfriend, and her father's significant other did not want her because she was jealous of the attention she got from her father. Her brothers were involved with drugs, and things were generally difficult. Mara, who was then sixteen, brought the girl home with her to live with us—at least until things were better for her—and that turned into almost two years. On the one hand, it was a surprise for us. On the other hand and to be consistent with the values we had instilled in Mara, how could we tell her that we couldn't be involved or shouldn't help?

It turned out to be a difficult but great experience. Mara's friend valued our family life and ended up being the first in her family to go to college. Mara learned that it wasn't always easy to do the right thing, as taking responsibility like this was both a full-time commitment and not always appreciated in the moment. We also learned together that doing the right thing had its ultimate benefits.

Today, Mara and her husband still volunteer a lot, taking in Midshipmen from the Naval Academy (near her house in Maryland) for weekends and holidays when they have circumstances that prevent them from going home— kind of parents-in-residence.

My husband and I have always supported a variety of causes and have been motivated to help and be active in our own community and in those around the world. It became a standing joke that my husband was the group husband for the single women at work when it came to helping them assess a real estate transaction, find a good mortgage, buy a car, or do their taxes! He was always willing to share his legal expertise and experience with those who needed the help (and at seventy-seven, he still does).

My own activism to make a difference made me want to instill that value in my company. I have always tried to emphasize purpose beyond profits. This philosophy drives us as a company. While being profitable is essential to rewarding staff, creating a sustainable business, and compensating shareholders, a business also needs a soul. The "why" of being in business needs to also be about significance and making a difference. It's about adding value to your clients beyond the obvious, and it's also about giving back in various ways as you can. This is not just about money, which for many small or medium-size enterprises is at a premium, but it is also about how you conduct business and what you do with the platform you have created to give something back to society through actions, ideas, and volunteering. I hope this emphasis is much more inspiring for staff as well, as they see that our company can and does make an impact every day.

Given that APCO is a majority woman-owned firm and the largest one globally in its field, championing the progress of women and girls globally has become part of APCO's DNA. We have created and promoted a number of programs around the world that advance the education of girls and women, focus on economic inclusion and gender equity, and encourage others to contribute to the effort.

As the chair of the Women Presidents' Organization, I have had the opportunity to work with more than two thousand woman-owned enterprises globally as they scale their businesses. While hosting their New York chapters, many of our younger women have been exposed to some of these dynamic women and hopefully have gained from the experience.

For the past several years, we have also had the opportunity to partner with the Graça Machel Trust in South Africa to help develop a program called Women Advancing Africa, bringing together some of the most fantastic women across the continent in a series of activities to help bring down barriers for the next generation of African women to thrive. It has been an honor to get to know these women and work with people like Ms. Machel, one of the most inspiring women I have met, and her trust's now former CEO, Nomsa Daniels.

As I prepare to pass the torch to a new generation, we have talked a lot about living our values of inclusion and diversity internally while continuing to take on things that make a difference in the world in which we live in addition to the work that is important to our day-to-day business. We hope this work will both inspire our staff and define our significance as a firm. That, to me, will be a fulfillment of a vision and passion that started at home, and I hope it will be a legacy to my children and grandchildren, as well as the staff at work.

People won't remember me, but hopefully, they will remember the programs that we helped put in place and the difference those programs make in people's lives. That's why my name isn't on the door, and I wouldn't want it there.

CHAPTER SEVEN

Lesson Seven:
Set Clear Boundaries—
Carrot and Stick

THE phrase "carrot and stick" is a metaphor for the use of a combination of reward and punishment to bring about desired behaviors. It is based on the idea that a cart driver might motivate a reluctant mule or horse to move forward by dangling a carrot in front of it rather than smacking the animal on the rear with a stick.

It's interesting that this ancient concept is so relevant today both for child-rearing and career development in the workplace.

With kids, it's easy to think of scores of examples where we as parents try to bring about a desired behavior or action. When they are little, children can be swayed by candy, a special toy, screen time, a visit to the park, or a special event to "behave" to get the reward later. While this isn't the most effective way to bring about good behavior in our children, we've all done it.

As our kids become older, it's definitely trickier. We

have to teach them lessons about life all along the way, and we can't learn the lesson for them. While we would all like our children to benefit from our experiences and life lessons, it does not work that way.

It sounds easy to just lay it out for them. If you study hard, you'll get good grades; good grades help you go to good schools; excellent schools help you prepare to get a quality job; great experience builds successful careers; *and* you can meet someone special along the way. There, done—a successful life! Well, we all know it's not that simple, that we have to help them with bite-size pieces of advice along the way, teaching the kids that life has its ups and downs, triumphs and failures. Helping them cope with the ups and downs, especially the downs, is an important part of building self-esteem and providing life skills.

And the "stick" is always there when punishment is necessary, but it is never something we as parents relish. It is important for our kids to experience reprimand in order to learn and grow. When they do something wrong, they must understand that there are consequences for those choices. Not physical punishment, but a change in privilege. If we don't enforce that discipline, it is hard to teach values, to have kids understand right from wrong.

There are no perfect parents, no perfect children, but that doesn't mean we don't strive to be the best parents and expect our children to be their best, always. When we disappoint each other, it hurts. Open communication about how we feel helps make it less likely there will be a repeat of the "offense."

The same is just as important or more important when something is done really well, even if it is something small. These are moments that build confidence and self-esteem. Some people are just not good or natural at giving compliments, especially when it is for something you think should be automatic or just common sense. That is why we have to pay particular attention to both the acts of praise as well as those of reprimand.

As parents, it's important that we provide a steady environment for our children so they understand the rules of what we expect of them and the consequences of decisions that deviate from the rules we have set. If the rules and our behavior are constantly changing, the kids will be confused and won't know how to behave. They need a guideline, a blueprint. We also have to walk the talk ourselves. It is *not* a matter of do as I say, but rather a matter of do as I do!

I truly believe that the consistency of parents' behavior helps build respect in their children and that children follow their parents' rules not only out of respect and perhaps a bit of fear of the consequences, but also love. Now, that love is constantly tested, as any parent knows. The kids understand the boundaries of behavior, and for the most part, they respect them, even though there are continual tests of the limits, which is all part of growing up.

Just as we are consistent with our children, we make sure the rules are well communicated to employees. We have to set clear rules and expectations so that employees understand what is expected of them and they understand the boundaries. Employees also want to know they are working in a company where there is consistency and fair application of the rules. Like siblings in a family, they watch to see if rules are equally applied and they have an equal opportunity to succeed, be promoted, be praised when something is good and that those who do not follow the rules or do their share are also dealt with in an even way.

Of course, unlike our children, for rule-breaking breeches of conduct, staff can be fired. But the harder part in dealing with employees is when offenses are not so obvious nor warrant termination. Those are the bigger tests. Are people held to the same standard of performance? Is there equal pay for equal work? Are the expectations clear? Is there honest feedback at review time? Is there a chance for input? Are you soliciting feedback that helps you be a better leader or manager? Do you walk the talk? To be honest, it is easier to understand when there is a clear breech of policy. It is a lot harder to have a consistent way of dealing with "problem children" who are just not aligned with policy, doing their job but undermining the company. It is amazing, however, that others not only notice, but are relieved when action is taken. Just as no one wants to be in a dysfunctional family, no one wants to see dysfunction where they work.

I've always tried to teach my kids that there are so many opportunities out there, but they need to take them, doing the hard work required to achieve those opportunities. Hard work has its own reward.

Early on, one of the ways I put the carrot in front of my kids—and now grandkids—was the ten-year-old trip. I'll talk more about this later in the book, but it was a way for the kids to spend time with me (and in most cases, my husband) one on one and travel to learn lessons about life and business. When they reach ten years old, I take them on an experience of their choosing, often in other parts of the world. The trips encourage learning, discipline, manners, and good behavior and teach them about planning for and achieving goals. The kids also get to travel and see amazing places, as you will see. These trips are planned by the kids themselves and are part of the experience of finding their interests and celebrating a milestone—kind of "career development" at an early age. I hope these trips and the other experiences I have built at home provide a launching pad for their growth, aspirations, and longer-term development as independent thinkers who appreciate and value the relationships they build and the opportunities they have.

I believe, beyond pay, that career development is the "carrot" for staff in the workplace. One of my greatest professional joys has been to mentor the most fantastic young professionals and see them grow and spread their wings. Many have advanced within our company and are today's leaders, building on a legacy I started but taking it to new and better levels. It gives me great satisfaction to watch this process and celebrate their success. Others have taken their experience at APCO and moved to other important positions in government, at other companies, in academia, and more. I often run into them on my business travels, and it is great that they feel their experience at APCO prepared them for interesting careers as they have moved on and there is still a sense of APCO in their hearts.

My job as leader is to provide a vision for where we are going and the values we share. Beyond that, I need to assure a comfortable, equitable, and challenging place to work. Since work can often be intense, I also need to make sure that we operate in an adult fashion and trust our employees to be fair and honest with us as well. This kind of mutual trust enables us to have a more flexible work environment to allow staff to handle their personal needs and provide plenty of opportunities for career development. I expect employees to take responsibility for themselves, kind of be their own boss in regard to the manner in which they work, and work with us to choose their own adventure. APCO can help serve up the smorgasbord of opportunity, but employees have to come to the table and serve themselves.

What do I mean by that?

Beyond creating a great work environment, we try to give staff individual flexibility to set their schedules. For example, if someone has to take their kids to school and gets in after 9:00 a.m., we don't care as long as the work is done. Good employees work hard to keep that flexibility and respect the trust we place in them. Those that take advantage shouldn't be here.

Given this flexibility, staff have to pace themselves. If they decide that they just are having a nonproductive day and they slack off, it's on them to catch up. If they can't, they become overloaded and miserable. The first consequence of slacking off is the inability to catch up, as the work doesn't stop. If you don't do your best to complete your work one day, you have no idea what you may walk into the next. Slackers can find themselves in impossible situations of their own making.

I look for people who are self-starters, who don't need to be told to do the work but just get on with it. If staff want global experience, I encourage them to apply to work on global programs. If an individual's passion is for research, nothing is stopping him or her from asking for work in that area.

I tell people to contribute at multiple levels, reaching out to departments beyond their own. I hate buckets and silos. We are an integrated firm, and there is nothing that prevents staff from reaching beyond their day-to-day environments to gain additional experience—the concept of freedom within the rules. *You know what you have to do, you know your responsibility to others, and you know your personal obligations. You should have the good judgment to make that work and, if you need help, to ask for it.* That's what I mean by an adult workplace. It is also how my husband and I ran our home.

We created a wonderful program, APCO-Plus, which is for entry-level staff. These "young people," as I call them, aren't assigned to any one practice group or task, and they get pulled into a variety of projects. I love to go to the area where they work, as the energy is palpable. I feel it and feed off of it.

So we put the carrot in front of our staff to entice them to learn and grow. We give them flexibility and a great work environment. If they don't take advantage, we counsel them. If they don't work hard and achieve for our clients, they are gone. Perhaps they need a rigidly structured environment to be successful, and that isn't our firm.

I have seen the carrot and stick work with client projects too. I am involved in the World Economic Forum's anti-corruption community, and we swiftly understood that countries don't want lectures on anti-corruption steps they should take. They are more inclined to take those steps if there is recognition for their efforts and the payoff is more interest in investment in their country. So, while standing firm on the principles that needed to be advanced, we adopted the idea of naming and faming those who did it right rather than naming and shaming those who didn't. The carrot became a great incentive to avoid the stick!

CHAPTER EIGHT

Lesson Eight:
Because I Said So Doesn't Cut It

LONG before I was leading teams of people, I was a young mother. Lisa, my oldest daughter, always wanted to know the rationale behind everything. I could never make her do anything unless she understood the reason. It was through this experience with Lisa that I learned early on that telling kids to do something because I said they should just didn't cut it. I needed to be patient—even when there was no time to do so—and explain the "why" every time, even if I got asked an endless series of questions as I explained.

As a result, I got into the habit, at home and at work, of explaining the "why" if I wanted my kids and grandkids or people at the office to follow my direction.

This practice rubbed off on my kids. When my youngest, Mara, was a teenager and couldn't drive yet, she wanted to go to a camp party with older kids. I was concerned that there would be drinking and then driving on difficult-to-navigate roads on the way home, so I said no.

Mara did not want to accept my answer and demanded that I explain why.

When I told her my concerns about drinking and driving, she worked on a solution. She found a friend to stay with near the camp so there wouldn't be a long drive home, and she promised me that there would be no drinking. She found a way to deal with my objections, so I gave in. She made me explain the "why not" and broke down my objections. Smart girl. It is the same way she continues to address situations today, providing clever alternatives to make smart choices.

So these early experiences with my kids probably shaped the kind of manager and leader I became. I have always tried to explain the "why" to staff so they understand why they need to do something in a certain way or the greater context for the assignment they receive. The downside of this approach is that explaining the rationale all the time can slow things down, but the benefits are so worth it. The end product is better. The staff develops peripheral vision and can better contribute to the client and often spot things that are outside the scope of the assignment they received but add greater value to the whole.

To institutionalize your mission, vision, values, ethics, and your business goals becomes easier when you are able to point to them to help explain the "why" and "how" things are done.[1]

---

[1] APCO's Mission, Values, and Operating Principles can be found on page 149.

Making these things live and breathe helps staff under-stand that they are really operating principles that are meaningful. I know of a CEO who consistently and fre-quently spoke of the company mission and values in just about everything he did, internally and externally. It was meaningful to staff, and they took the mission and values very seriously, incorporating them into their own goals and work.

When the next CEO came in and didn't do the same thing, employees were left to wonder if he took the mission and values seriously and if certain types of behavior would be tolerated. The staff actually missed the frequent refer-ences to the mission and values and noted so in the annual employee survey. Staff like consistency, just like kids do.

There are a number of side benefits to taking the time to explain your rationale or your vision. None of us are as smart as all of us, I like to say. When you take the time to explain the greater context or the reason for doing some-thing, often it inspires good ideas for new projects or for implementing the task at hand. This is true especially in a consulting environment where you work on teams. The more those teams work in silos, the less likely they are to have creative and thoughtful solutions.

Not every decision you make in life is going to be pop-ular, whether at home or at work, so taking action without explaining the "why" can make people confused and angry. While explanations don't always come with agreement on the decision, they do help people understand the rationale for the decision. Sometimes, as in Mara's case, it results in doing something one otherwise would not have been given permission to do. Other times, it just takes the sting out of a decision that has been made or creates a platform for further discussion.

Dictators are rarely successful at work or at home. Many times, that means you must slow things down and explain your rationale, particularly when assigning tasks that may—on the surface—send confusing signals.

"Do this because I said so" isn't a winning strategy to inspire your staff or motivate your kids, so think about sharing the "why" and see if it works for you. You may be surprised!

CHAPTER NINE

Lesson Nine:
Show Where There's a Will,
There's a Way

THE saying "where there's a will, there's a way" has been around for a long time. Its origin dates back to 1640 when it was stated: *To him that will, ways are not wanting.* The phrase was modernized and appeared as we know it in *New Monthly Magazine* in 1822. For such an old phrase, I believe it's still relevant and holds a lot of promise for achievement today. The saying encourages us to be persistent in achieving our goals and dreams. And in my case, I wouldn't have achieved what I have without believing that if you want something bad enough, you can make it happen, even when everyone says you can't.

Trust me, if I listened to everyone who told me what I couldn't do, I would become discouraged and give up. This inner voice has kept reminding me *not* to accept limitations imposed by others.

My mother was the one who made this old saying my mantra as she taught me to continue to work to achieve my goals every step along the way, even when others told me I couldn't. You have to remember that I grew up in the 50s and 60s when women were told what they couldn't do quite frequently. And it is especially interesting that this came from my mother, who often allowed the opinions of others to feed her insecurity. I guess, in retrospect, she is someone who faced a lot of obstacles in her life but never complained about them. She left Poland at age four and ended up in Cuba, where she grew up. As she got older and realized that there were limited opportunities in Cuba under the dictator Fulgencio Batista, she came to the United States as a young woman on her own and made a life in the US. This must have required a lot of determination that I never gave her credit for until I was old enough to understand.

Thanks to the encouragement from my mother, from the time I was a young girl, I believed that anything was possible. Because this belief was embedded in my soul, I continued to crash through obstacles personally and professionally. Sure, there were times when the obstacles were too much and things didn't work out as I had hoped, but I tend to focus on the many times that I was able to achieve something that I was repeatedly told I couldn't do.

When people said I couldn't go to college without finishing my high school diploma, I did. When I went to work at the start of Close Up with two small kids, I made it work. When I started my own company when I was married and had three kids, so many told me that I couldn't do it. I did. And when I ran my company differently than others I was told:

You are doing everything the wrong way.

You can't do that as a woman.

You can't operate the company that way. You'll never get to scale.

You can't operate without more command and control.

But we did.

I am a glass-half-full person. That is just who I am. I always believe that something can be accomplished, even if it takes all night to do it. I believe in the possible, and I always will. I hope I have been a role model to my children and to my staff in showing the way that things can be done —how they can be accomplished even though those things may have seemed impossible at the start. Obviously, none of this happens in a vacuum. I think one reason I've had a fifty-plus-year marriage is that I don't consider failure an option. I am not sure that Steve always thought the same things were possible, but he pitched in and believed in and supported my determination. I would not have had the capacity and fortitude to do this if my spouse were not my biggest cheerleader.

To be honest, I have also tried to surround myself at work with people who share the same commitment and passion to get things done, to find the way to achieve goals despite obstacles. I don't have a lot of patience or tolerance for those who always start by saying why things won't work. I believe there is always a path and that you at least have to try. It is something I am not sure our clients even understand, but when we agree to do something, I believe we have a duty to keep thinking about it and working on it until we make the impossible possible.

I have been blessed over the years with hundreds of people who have believed in my view of making things happen. When I started the company, there were lots of people who left good careers and good jobs to join something that was really a figment of imagination. When we dreamed of being a ten-million-dollar business, people thought it was crazy, but we met and passed our goal way ahead of schedule. Then we set the next goal post. Today, we are in more than twenty countries with almost thirty offices and have our sights set on the one-hundred-fifty-million mark for revenues. All of this is powered by a belief in ourselves and the underlying philosophy that if we will it and work hard, we can make it happen.

In forming and building a new enterprise, you need to have passionate people around you who believe in your mission and are willing to put in the time and effort to make your company a success, despite roadblocks. Some of those roadblocks can prove to be almost fatal. But believing in yourself and not taking no for an answer goes a long way in smashing obstacles and achieving success. APCO has been built on the spirit of those who help smash the obstacles and press forward, even when, at times, they don't think it is possible. Their spirit and support has been my greatest gift, and hopefully, the success is their reward.

Kids watch their parents and their grandparents. They take note of some of the things that may not be obvious at the time. Living a life of drive and purpose is a powerful lesson. Life has a lot of ups and downs, and having the will to push forward is a life skill that has many rewards over time. I guess I never really realized this. It just came naturally as a result of the way I was raised. I watch my children and am amazed by the things they do and then have an inward smile because I realize they, too, are strong-willed and find ways to make things happen.

In preparing for this book, I interviewed my grandchildren about their ten-year-old trips—discussed in the next chapter—and was very surprised when Nina, the first one to go, said she learned a lot from watching me "in action" on the trip. You see, she chose London for the trip, and when it was time to go home, we couldn't. A volcano had erupted in Iceland, and the ash cloud caused the London airport and most of those in Western Europe to shut down. Over the next few days, we had a marathon trip to Brussels and then Paris in search of an open airport with an available flight. Even though we were told there were none, I kept at it and managed to get us a flight home from Paris while the London airport was still closed. I also got us upgraded, which was the icing on the cake.

For me, it was business as usual and I was on a mission. But I guess for Nina, to whom I was Grandma, it was a lesson in finding a way to make something happen that everyone was saying was impossible. I barely remember making a big deal of this, but Nina is now nineteen and was sharing her view about this as a highlight of lessons learned on her trip.

This is the same Nina who is always full of good ideas, starting from her earliest days—a photocopy of her mother's precociousness at the same age. One day I remarked to Nina, a six-year-old, "Where do all those good ideas come from?" She looked me straight in the eye and told me she had an idea machine in her brain and they just kept popping out. I thought I would be a supportive grandparent and enthusiastically told her that was terrific and asked, "Where do I get one?" She got very serious and sad and told me, "You have to be born with it. Either you have it, or you don't!" I guess I redeemed myself on her trip, but this little story is always a reminder that people either have a can-do attitude or they don't. My life has been blessed by knowing people who make things happen because they refuse to fail. Lots of those people have been attracted to APCO over the years, and I like to think this positive spirit and passion is a big differentiator for the firm. Thanks, Nina!

Parents are role models to their children by example, so by demonstrating commitment to meet challenging goals and overcome obstacles, parents encourage children to move outside of their comfort zones to explore and achieve and be creative about how they approach life's problems. The same is true in the workplace when leaders set the example for staff by persisting to achieve critical goals, particularly for clients.

"Where there's a will, there's a way" is not an archaic

phrase to me; it is a way of life and, wherever possible, a business promise. I hope I have demonstrated to my family and colleagues at work that I embrace this in a way that has inspired them to persist in achieving their own goals, personally and professionally.

Nina, Margery's first grandchild, rides the London Eye on her ten-year-old trip that she took with her grandparents in 2010. The Icelandic ash cloud delayed their return to the US, creating an adventure to conclude the trip. Nina is now a college student at Carnegie Mellon University in Pittsburg.

Margery, Nina, and Steve got diverted to Paris because of the Icelandic ash cloud in 2010. Not a bad detour!

Margery and her nine grandkids on a family outing in Cancun, Mexico, on New Year's Day in 2019.

Margery's father, Sol, at age 90, with Margery and Steve's grandchildren, his great grandchildren. He lived with Margery and Steve for several years until he died at age 93 in 2013.

CHAPTER TEN

Lesson Ten:
Expand Horizons
and the Ten-Year-Old Trip

FROM the time I was quite young, I have felt like a citizen of the world. Traveling around the globe for work and pleasure is my lifeblood. The passion for learning about different cultures and exploring new places probably was cemented when I was sixteen and served as a nanny in Austria. I got to travel around Europe on my own and was immediately hooked.

As I started my business, I began to realize that people are the same almost everywhere. If you give them something in which to believe, they are excited to be part of it. I have had a spectacular opportunity to get to know some fantastic people during my thirty-five years of building APCO. Many have become like family. I have had the joy and pride of watching them grow as professionals, and whether staying at APCO or moving to other challenges, they have found a way to make a difference.

As I have gotten older and reflected on this, I have come to realize that some of the same things that have made our family a cohesive unit are very similar to those that have formed the fabric of the company: an articulated set of values—the roots—and freedom to operate within a defined framework with the encouragement to stretch and continue to explore new ways to do things and new ideas that keep you motivated and fresh—the wings.

While every business is motivated to give a financial return to those who have invested time and cash, I have always felt that APCO should do more. We should use our platform as a force for good. Part of being a good business is being a positive contributor to society. I am proud that the company has been able to be a successful business while providing flexibility to get involved in things that we think important. I have felt that mandate is especially important in regard to advancing women across the globe. Perhaps it is a way to share the good fortune that I have enjoyed. I often reflect that as a child of immigrants, I not only have had a fantastic opportunity, but I should also have a responsibility to those less fortunate.

It is a value system that also has shaped the values of my kids and now my grandchildren. Be curious about the world, be caring about those who do not have the same opportunities that you do, and push the boundaries of your comfort zone.

One way I have tried to instill these values is to lead by example. So when my kids were growing up, I thought it would be great to have them see what I did and why I was gone when I had to travel. And so the ten-year-old trip was born. Originally, the age was arbitrary, but it was a fixed time when each of the kids would know they would go with their mother on a business trip and get to spend some one-on-one time. They each had an identical trip—to Denver, Colorado, for meetings and then into the mountains to Estes Park so they could experience the majesty of the Rockies and see some of the American West. Each of these trips meant a lot to me, and I learned later how influential they were in the lives of each of my children. The trips also helped me understand the real meaning of work-life integration.

It wasn't until thirty-one years later that I fully understood how much these trips meant to my children. When my oldest daughter, Lisa, participated in the trip, she never really talked a lot about it. It wasn't until her daughter was nine that I came to appreciate that it must have made an impression because Nina, Lisa's oldest child, called me just before her tenth birthday to announce to me that she was going to be ten on her next birthday (as if a grandmother is not tracking this!). When I told her that it was natural to turn ten after being nine, she immediately got impatient with me and said, "I know that, Grandma, but it is time for my ten-year-old trip!" This was something we had never discussed, and there could only have been one source for this—her mother. So thirty-one years later, I learned that it had indeed had the intended consequences.

Nina's influence didn't end there. While I was recovering from her reference to the ten-year-old trip, she announced that she couldn't decide if she wanted to go to Russia or China, two places that I traveled to quite a bit at the time. When I explained that her mother had gone to Colorado, she told me, "Times have changed."

In the end and after some negotiation, Nina went to London. When my husband and I agreed to this trip, we had no idea that it would make such a difference in our lives. Nina, being Nina, spent time preparing and had a list of things that she wanted to do in London. I thought it would be interesting for her to see the London APCO office but also to meet other kids from the UK, so we invited all the ten-year-old daughters of APCO's London office to join us for an evening out. One of the girls, Chiara Walsh, bonded immediately with Nina and ended up staying with her for a good part of the trip, making it especially fun for Nina.

While I knew Nina would enjoy the trip, what I never expected was what this trip would do for my husband and me. Seeing London through the eyes of a ten-year-old was truly special—even though I had been to London more than thirty times. Even more important, spending that quality time with Nina was so special; it cemented a bond for a lifetime. Steve and I realized that we started a tradition that would forever impact our lives. Time proved that we were right and that we had created something very special, giving us insight into the unique character of each of our grandchildren. It also created legacy moments that we will take to the grave.

As you will see, these trips were not about where we went, but rather, it was about having an experience shaped by each of the grandchildren. As we went along, each of the kids did a lot of research in advance to help plan their trip. It is great to be a co-conspirator with them. It is really fun both to spend the quality time and to have this unique experience.

Nina set a precedent, and over time, we made sure we allocated enough time for each experience. Many people have now told us that they are "stealing" this idea. We welcome and encourage that and emphasize that it is not about how far you go or how much money is spent. It is about the bonding time and the quality of the experience together and the engagement that precedes it. In fact, just as I was finishing this book and on the road, I received a call from my oldest grandson, David. We were planning an outing to a basketball game in a couple of weeks, and he commented that he was looking forward to the "alone time" with Grandma (quite an admission for a fifteen-year-old boy). And as we talked about our mutual enthusiasm about our outing, he brought up his ten-year-old trip and told me that he might not have realized it at the time, but as he reflected on it, he focused on how special it was and how the memories flood back from time to time. He especially commented on how fortunate he was to be exposed to so many new things that stay with him as he grows up.

Back to Nina.

She got more than she bargained for. When we were scheduled to go home, the Icelandic volcano erupted and closed the airports in Europe for several days. As a result, we went in search of an airport, and Nina—poor Nina—got to see Brussels and Paris before we finally caught a flight from Paris, providing extra drama for all of us and also introducing Nina to a broad swath of APCO teammates in three countries who helped us along the way. Upon her return home, her mother wrote a song about the trip, which her whole family would perform. Some of the lyrics are included below.

"Nina Went to London"
by Lisa Edwards

Nina went to London, 'cause she thought it would be fun then
Eyjafjallajokull erupted, spewing ash.
She went to see the Union Jack but didn't know if she'd get back
And all the tourists wound up spewing cash.

CHORUS:
Stateside nerves frayed by the hour
As the kid was touring London Tower.
Though London Bridge, it didn't fall,
The airplanes couldn't fly at all.

And high above the London Eye,
She couldn't hear her mother's cry:
"Forget the double decker bus
And come back home to us."

Lisa, her husband, and kids are all very musical, and the whole family plays instruments and sings. Hearing Lisa and

Nina perform this song was so much fun, helping us recall and laugh about this eventful trip.

During the holidays, I interviewed my grandkids and asked them to comment on their ten-year-old trips. Some of the key points followed certain themes: they appreciated the one-on-one time; wanted to learn and experience something new; enjoyed taking risks and challenging themselves; experienced the beauty in meeting new people and appreciated the bonds I had with the various members of the APCO team if they visited a local office; and had their eyes opened to the wonder of discovering a different place and/or culture.

I thought it might be instructive to hear from the grandchildren directly. As I said before, our very first grandchild ten-year-old trip was with our granddaughter, Nina, who is now at Carnegie Mellon. My husband, Steve, was able to make the trip as well and has been an important part of most of the rest of the trips. Nina learned that travel doesn't always go smoothly.

Here is what Nina had to say about her trip:

"I was the first to go outside the country. I had never been to another continent, and I thought going to London was cool, as I could still speak the language and was able to interact with people, learning more about the place. Traveling without parents and the bonding time with grandparents was a big deal. The trip was a rite of passage. Getting to see Grandma working hard and then seeing the impact of her work was interesting.

"Traveling is not always a luxury. Something happens that is not always planned. How calm Grandma had to be in a crisis, taking things in stride. It was a pretty remarkable thing. In retrospect, it was very hard, and I didn't realize at the time how many others were stuck. We got extra travel, took the Eurostar, and saw the Eiffel Tower! Grandma's resolution was an amazing thing. To see how this crisis was handled was useful in my own life. Remain calm in the storm. The whole experience made me strive to be a leader."

Years later, our seventh grandchild, Ian, went with us to Iceland and let me know that one of the highlights of his trip was to see the volcano that caused Nina to get stuck in Europe! Interesting how this came full circle and how interested they have been in each other's experiences. Ian also added that going snowmobiling and into the lava caves was a highlight, in spite of the fact that Grandma got thrown from the snowmobile and ended up having surgery.

Our granddaughter, Brennan, went with us to Italy. She had always wanted to steer a gondola in Venice. But we encouraged her to start in Rome so there could be more history built into the trip. Brennan visited the APCO office in Rome. She's the one who got curious about the Italian elections that had just taken place and actually discussed Italian politics with the staff.

Here is her reflection on the trip:

"Going to Italy put me in a place where I could re-late to other countries, experience other cultures, and see people who are different. My dad influenced my choice because he had been a lot of places. So I thought: what is a place that is memorable and where I would go back again? Happy I chose Italy. I got to steer a gondola myself—something I always wanted to do.

"The trip gave me a push to open up to other places and better relate to history class and more things in life. Maybe it's easier for me to adapt now because I experienced all of this at a young age."

Just like my three kids, all of my grandkids are different, with their own distinct personalities. My granddaughter, Dagny—who is more cautious, did not want to travel outside of the United States but wanted to go about as far away as she could—chose California. She was so funny and said, "I was an anxious ten-year-old. I didn't want to leave the country."

She absolutely loved going to San Francisco. She was moved by Alcatraz and enjoyed walking along Pier 39, spotting the sea lions. We also explored the redwood forest. She admitted that she was a bit intimidated by the trip.

Dagny said:

"I was apprehensive at first, but then I let go and had fun, learning that I could do things on my own. The trip helped me challenge myself. You don't have to go

far to see beautiful things. You don't have to go places too extreme to see things that are important or interesting. It all translates to life."

Our granddaughter, Ainsley, loves animals, and that was an important part of consideration for her ten-year-old trip. Her ultimate fantasy was to go on safari and see lots of animals. She lucked out, as I had undertaken a project with the Graça Machel Trust, and we were doing an inaugural meeting in South Africa. So, in consultation with Ainsley, we decided that she would go with me and her grandfather to South Africa a week early to go to my meetings, and then we would all go on a safari. The safari alone was a terrific experience. We got to see all the "Big Five"[2] and had one of the most fantastic experiences of our lives—grandparents and grandchild.

But what was extra special was meeting Nelson Mandela's widow. In preparation, Ainsley read all about Mr. Mandela, Graça Machel, and apartheid. She visited Soweto, saw Mandela's house, and learned about what happened to kids her own age during this period. Best of all, she spent time with Ms. Machel, who left a lasting impression on Ainsley.

On the subject of Graça Machel, Ainsley said, "It was really cool to meet someone I had read about . . . I was

---

[2] In Africa, the Big Five game animals are the lion, leopard, rhinoceros (both black and white species), elephant, and Cape buffalo. The term "big five game" was coined by big-game hunters and refers to the five most difficult animals in Africa to hunt on foot.

really excited, and it is something I will remember for the rest of my life."

In addition to meeting Graça Machel and going on safari, she explored the region with her grandfather while I finished my meetings. That also left an impression on Ainsley.

She said:

"To go to the cradle of mankind helped me in social studies. The trip kept me focused. I can do so much more than I ever thought I could. It was a fun time to be with my grandparents without my parents. And to go to cool places that I picked myself without my sisters and brother!"

Elijah, now thirteen, decided, of all the places in the world, he wanted to go to Mount Rushmore. As much as we do not try to influence the trip, in this case, we felt that we needed to build something meaningful around this wish. After research, that is exactly what we did. We took an overnight train to Utah from Chicago and then joined a prearranged Amtrak tour, going through the Tetons and Yosemite and ending—you guessed it—at Mount Rushmore.

Elijah was a fantastic travel companion and made friends with everyone, including many senior citizens. He was like a celebrity. In fact, at the banquet on the last night, almost everyone had a comment about Elijah and how great it was to have him on the trip. He was just about the only child and was adopted by all and actually helped to build a real spirit in the group.

Elijah recalled his favorite parts of the trip:

"The most fun was sleeping on the train, seeing Mount Rushmore, and all the things I learned about the national parks. I became a Junior Ranger!

"To have individual time with my grandparents, NOT with all the other cousins, was great and a very personal experience for me."

And, because some things just happen, we really lucked out. The day we went to Mount Rushmore, the last surviving member of the team that built Mount Rushmore, Nick Clifford (who is now ninety-eight), had just published his book and was signing them in the gift shop. Elijah had the opportunity to sit down for a chat, get the book, and learn even more about this interesting place.

David, now fifteen, chose to go to Galapagos. I didn't know much about this destination, but David had done all the research and gave us a full itinerary. In asking David about his trip, he said that the whole thing was a fantastic experience, but he especially thought that going somewhere so different made him more adventurous about going to new places and trying new things. His favorite memory is actually a memory that I will take to my grave. He and I were snorkeling and looked down, and we were swimming above a family of sharks! David looked at me wide-eyed, and I got a big thumbs-up. We still talk about that magic moment.

My granddaughter, Leighton, will be the next to go, followed by our youngest grandchild, Kiley. As I mentioned earlier, Leighton had encephalitis when she was two years old. Her mother was fighting a very serious bout of breast cancer at the same time, and I have an image seared in my brain of Leighton's limp body in her bald mother's arms in the hospital. Needless to say, this was a terrible time for our family.

Both are well now, thank goodness. But since I can remember, she has been talking about her ten-year-old trip, and now that she is ten, she is starting to do research to choose among locations for her trip. Her musings to date include going to Milan for Milan Fashion Week with an empty suitcase! She has always had her own style, and I guess she knows more about this than I do.

According to Leighton, she is very excited. "I just love fashion, and I will learn so much. I am also excited to go with my grandparents because they won't say no to the things I want to do . . ." (She does get her way with Papa). "I also look forward to being the only child."

And Kiley, now nine, is beginning to think about where she will go. It's fun to watch her talk through her ideas with her cousins and narrow her choices. She is clear about one thing: animals will be involved.

I debated about including the adventures of the ten-year-old trip in this book about running my business, but truthfully, I learned so much about myself, my family, and my relationship with my work that I could not resist.

Ultimately, these trips reminded me about what is important in life and the power of personal experience. This is something that has definitely impacted my work and the environment I hope that I create. We have exposed many of our younger staff to their first trip abroad, their first time at an iconic site, their first meeting with a head of state or celebrity, and many other life-changing experiences. It is my personal hope that everyone who comes to APCO has something special in their experience that they can reflect on with pride and that creates a life memory.

As I look back on my career, first at Close Up and then my thirty-five years building APCO, I have been truly blessed with these kinds of life-altering experiences. While they have definitely made my life richer and made me better at what I do, I think the most important lesson I have learned is not to take my success or myself too seriously. I have seen a lot of people over the years in the rise of their careers and the sense of self-importance that can come with it, and I have also seen them after their time in the limelight.

The one constant that has grounded me is family. Family keeps me balanced and reminds me of the core values of life. It is hard to take yourself seriously if you are baking brownies with your twelve-year-old grandchild, making smiley-face pancakes on the weekend, carving the Thanksgiving turkey, or doing household chores, for that matter. There is something very special about having fun with your kids or grandkids at an amusement park. For a while, you forget the seriousness of daily life and the responsibilities you hold. I think it is called perspective. And

I think that perspective is the underlying theme of this book.

Don't get me wrong. I take my responsibilities and my work very seriously. I feel responsible for building a strong and sustainable company where employees can count on their careers and support their families. I believe, as leaders, we get into trouble when we believe the hype and compliments we receive because we have positions of power. To repeat: We can't take ourselves too seriously. So I am enormously grateful that I have my family to make sure that I keep a healthy and balanced perspective and those at work who tell me what's *really* happening, rather than what they think I want to hear.

So I end where I started, with work/life integration. Find the path that gives you satisfaction and enables you to remember what is important, and be sure to share life's experiences with your fellow workers and your work experience with your family. Learn to laugh at yourself and to celebrate life. And when you have those down moments, remember that no one can make you feel inferior without your own consent.

Granddaughter Brennan with Margery and Steve as part of Brennan's ten-year-old trip to Italy. They visited Rome, Florence, and Venice in 2013.

In 2015, grandson Elijah choose Mount Rushmore for his trip, which included a train ride from Chicago.

Elijah with Nick Clifford, 95, the last surviving Mount Rushmore driller. Clifford signed one of his books for Elijah during his ten-year-old trip.

Granddaughter Dagny riding one of the famous cable cars in San Francisco in 2012.

Grandson David meets a friend on a trip to the Galapagos with his grandparents in 2014.

Grandson Ian and Steve on their way to Iceland as part of Ian's special ten-year-old trip with his grandparents in 2018.

Granddaughter Ainsley meeting Graça Machel, the widow of Nelson Mandela. Ainsley researched Ms. Machel and her husband prior to the trip. She also went on an African safari as part of her ten-year-old trip with her grandparents in 2016.

Margery and Steve with their kids and grandkids, celebrating their 50th anniversary in Alaska in 2016.

Margery's granddaughters, Leighton, left, and Kiley, right, in a photo from 2014. These two girls will be the last of Margery's grandchildren to go on their ten-year-old trips.

Kiley, 9, left, and Leighton, 10, in December, 2018. These two cousins are always hugging and conspiring about things, including their upcoming ten-year-old trips.

EPILOGUE

I am often asked to share the career advice I would give my younger self on lessons learned. Here goes.

Encourage optimism.

When we are young, we feel this unlimited potential—we can do anything, accomplish anything. Continue to fuel this optimism and see the unlimited opportunities in front of you throughout your life.

Not everyone is going to see life the way you do.

It's a hard truth when you learn that not all people are good people. You'll have your disappointments, particularly learning people you thought you could trust have deceived you.

You will work hard for people who will never appreciate it, but don't be cynical.

Just move on.

Don't overanalyze opportunities, as good things happen at inconvenient times.

I wasn't thinking of getting married at twenty years old. Steve was just one of the most decent people, and we shared a great deal in common. When I envisioned a life partner, Steve was it for me. Everyone thought I'd be the last person to get married, but Steve and I felt we would figure everything out.

For work opportunities, find those things that give you pleasure, help you grow as an individual, or that will help you expand the things you like to do. By the way, as you get older, those things become clearer. I wasn't looking to start a company when I had the opportunity to start APCO, as I was instrumental in building Close Up, wasn't looking to leave, and was emotionally attached. Here's the thing—once you move forward, you can't look back. While you can have pride in your past accomplishments, you have to turn the page. No regrets. The past is with you forever, your legacy, but you have to have a mindset that *this is my next adventure.* And don't compare your new opportunity to anything from the past. This is your new future.

Never underestimate the value of being underestimated.

My company dealt with a lot of senior officials, so I employed some very high-level people with world-class expertise. I was often the only woman in the room. A number of these men felt they could do a better job than I could. They thought I was too soft, as they were much more in "command and control" mode and I have always been more of a consensus builder, perhaps what some would say is a feminine trait. I chose to build my company culture on the values I started the company with, rather than base it on fear. I was constantly under scrutiny and directly criticized by people who should have been fired for their actions (and some didn't last very long!). If I took everything personally, I would have had my head in the sand and gone home in tears every night. What good is that?

What I learned was that if people are prejudiced or biased, use it to your advantage, because they will never see you coming. I can give you scores of examples of how I was able to come away with deals done and challenges accomplished just because I was able to outmaneuver those who underestimated me in some way. If people are blind to confidence and success, I am going to use it in a way that is helpful to what I want to accomplish.

Be more prepared to be heard.

Unfortunately, women still have to do this in many instances. I can ask women in business this question, and I know the answer: How many times have you said something really smart and no one listens, and then a man says the same thing and the consensus in the room is it's the best idea they have ever heard? You have to decide for yourself how you are going handle this, but in all cases, come to every meeting fully prepared and make sure your ideas are heard by speaking up.

Stand your ground against bad behavior.

In your career and life, there will be abusive people. It is tough to endure the mental abuse when you are demeaned, but you must stand up against this behavior. Yelling or shouting in kind never helps. Always be professional and make your point.

Create your network of colleagues and friends.

I have certain friends who give me joy just by being near them. Other friends are experts in their fields and can offer advice and test my judgment. Other friends don't take anything; they just give. I've found that the more you give, the more you get. This mosaic of fantastic relationships helps shape my life. Create your mosaic of friendships and relationships that enrich your life, both personally and professionally.

The ultimate reward in life and a career well spent has to come from inside you.

You must drive your own personal self-satisfaction. To be a happy and fulfilled person, you have to learn to reach inside and find that satisfaction within you; it doesn't come from others. We grow up, and a lot of times, we expect accolades or gratification to come from external sources. If you wait for that to come, you may be very disappointed in life.

Having a life partner is a gift that is not to be taken for granted.

Trying to balance family with career growth and development is difficult work, but the rewards far exceed the pain points and struggle. Treasure your partner and never take him or her for granted.

I hope the lessons I've learned in my life and work have been helpful. It's been a joy to share them with you!

About Margery Kraus

MARGERY KRAUS, founder and executive chairman of APCO Worldwide, a global advisory and advocacy communications consultancy headquartered in Washington, DC, specializes in public affairs, communication, and business consulting for major multinationals. Kraus founded APCO in 1984 and transformed it from a company with one small Washington office to a multinational consulting firm in major cities throughout the Americas, Europe, the Middle East, Africa, and Asia. In September 2004, Kraus led a management buyout of her firm, making APCO one of the largest privately owned consulting firms in its field in the world and the largest that is majority women owned. APCO was built almost entirely through organic growth. Throughout the years, Kraus achieved this by fusing the best local talent and experience with a global perspective and best practices, resulting in an international firm with a unique culture based on seamless teamwork and common values.

Kraus's achievements have been recognized over the years through a number of prestigious awards, including the Enterprising Women of the Year Award (2019); PRWeek Top 20 Most Influential Communicator (2018); PRWeek Hall of Femme (2017); PR News PR People Hall of Fame (2015); C200 Foundation Entrepreneurial Champion Award (2015); PRWeek Hall of Fame (2014); U.S. Association of Former Members of Congress Corporate Statesmanship Award (2013); Volunteers of America (Greater New York) Spirit of the Founders (2012); the Plank Center for Leadership in Public Relations Agency Mentorship (2012); Global Thinkers Forum Excellence in Leadership (2012); Arthur W. Page Society Hall of Fame (2011); Institute for Public Relations Alexander Hamilton Medal for lifetime contributions to professional public relations (2010); Washington Business Hall of Fame (2009); Enterprising Women Hall of Fame (2009); Ernst & Young Entrepreneur of the Year in the services category in Greater Washington (2006); Washington PR Woman of the Year (2006); and PR News Lifetime Achievement (2005).

Kraus specializes in providing strategic counsel on issue-based communication, crisis management, market entry, and corporate reputation across diverse industry groups. The range of her experience is reflected in APCO's industry practice groups. In addition, she pioneered one of the industry's earliest practices in corporate responsibility and the development of public/private partnerships.

Prior to starting APCO, Kraus assisted in the creation and development of the Close Up Foundation, a multimillion-dollar educational foundation sponsored in part by the United States Congress. Kraus continues to be involved with the foundation by serving on its board of directors.

Kraus is active on other institutional and corporate boards and committees. She is chairman of the board of the Women Presidents' Organization; serves on the international advisory board of Tikehau Capital, the social responsibility advisory board of Univision Communications Corporate, and the advisory board of *Enterprising Women* magazine. She also serves as a trustee of American University, the Catherine B. Reynolds Foundation, and the Institute for Public Relations. She previously served as a trustee for Northwestern Mutual for more than a decade. In addition, she is a past chairman of the Public Affairs Council and the board of directors of the PR Council. She also served on the advisory board of the J.L. Kellogg Graduate School of Management at Northwestern University, as well as the steering committee of the school's Center for Executive Women.

Kraus is the author of numerous articles in the fields of public affairs management and corporate reputation and has been a guest lecturer throughout the world. She holds a bachelor of arts and master of arts in political science and public law from American University.

She has been married to her husband, Steve, for more than fifty years, is a mother of three, and has nine grandchildren.

https://www.facebook.com/margerykrausauthor

About Phyllis J. Piano

PHYLLIS J. PIANO spent more than thirty years as an award-winning corporate communications expert for some of the world's largest companies. She is currently a member of APCO Worldwide's International Advisory Council. She and her husband split their time between California, England, and the Midwest. *Hostile Takeover: A Love Story,* her first novel, was published in October 2016. Her second book, *Love Reconsidered,* was published in 2017. As she is a world traveler, Piano's books were written and edited on three continents. When she is not packing a bag, making artisan sourdough bread, or cooking with lots of garlic, Piano is working on her next novel.

Learn more and connect with her at:

www.phyllispiano.com
Twitter: @ppiano
www.facebook.com/phyllisjpianoauthor/
www.instagram.com/phyllisjpiano/
www.linkedin.com/in/phyllis-j-piano

APCO'S MISSION, VALUES, AND OPERATING PRINCIPLES

APCO Worldwide strives to be a responsible company in everything we do. Our commitment to conducting our business at the highest level of ethics and integrity is derived from the core values that have guided us since our founding. This commitment is embodied in our Code of Conduct, which sets forth the fundamental ethical principles that govern how we do business.

Our commitment to operating responsibly includes acting with strong ethics and integrity; adhering to standards of good governance and financial stewardship; supporting our local communities; and managing our environmental footprint. We comply with local laws of every market in which we operate, adhere to industry codes of conduct to which we are a signatory, and strive to meet stakeholder expectations. We aim to serve clients who are committed to the same high standards of integrity and accountability.

OUR MISSION

In a rapidly evolving global context and a time of transformational change, APCO strives to add value to our clients' enterprises and benefit society. We enable clients to achieve their objectives through insightful counsel, authentic advocacy, and creative communications.

ACCOMPLISHING OUR MISSION

We accomplish our mission by hiring, retaining, and developing exceptional people from diverse backgrounds; engaging our people in thoughtful and challenging work; and fostering a culture of critical and unconventional thinking. We are committed to fostering diversity and inclusion by celebrating differences in our culture by race, gender, generation, religion, and geography, and our efforts have been recognized by our industry. As a certified woman-owned business, we are actively engaged in organizations that focus on the advancement of diversity in our industry as well across societies in which we operate.

We achieve results by acquiring a deep understanding of our clients' objectives and matching this with deep insights into their political, economic, and social environments and actionable strategic support.

By operating as one integrated company with offices around the world, we secure our clients' license to operate and grow by delivering results that are locally relevant and often globally impactful.

OUR VALUES

The values we put forth—to everyone throughout the organization—reflect our dual commitment to our people and our clients.

- **Boldness**: We push boundaries and produce better ideas to solve the really challenging problems of our time.

- **Inclusivity**: Our culture embraces diversity of people, thoughts, and experiences.

- **Curiosity**: We hunger for learning and improvement in all we do, keeping us at the cutting edge.

- **Empathy**: We seek to embrace and incorporate different customs and approaches and to understand the perspectives of others.

OPERATING PRINCIPLES

These business principles were part of our DNA long before they were put to paper.

- Make client success our measurement of achievement
- Empower people to do great work
- Nurture an organization where everyone is valued
- Rely on one another to achieve personal potential
- Build relationships to build business
- Tell the truth
- Push the boundaries with innovative technology and solutions
- Provide global service culture by culture

For more information, go to
WWW.APCOWORLDWIDE.COM

ACKNOWLEDGMENTS

This book would not have come about without the prodding, assistance, and support of Phyllis Piano. She is not only a dear friend, but also an experienced author and member of APCO's International Advisory Council. Lots of people have encouraged me to write a book about my experiences, but I have not yet been ready to do that. The idea of a book that is about work/life integration and what I have learned from family has always been something I have wanted to do.

I thought of it, but Phyllis jumped on it and helped me convert this idea into the pages you see in the book.

I also want to thank Brent Crane, who conspired with Phyllis to make sure I kept at it when I was delinquent with my drafts or feedback. His co-conspirator was none other than my daughter, Mara Hedgecoth, who has always had my back and helped to push me beyond my comfort zone when it comes to talking about myself.

Thanks to our editor, Cassie McCown, for her many contributions, including pushing for details on the most challenging times of my life.

As you might imagine, I rely on my family for lots of things, and this book is no exception. It is the loving support I have received over the years that has made my life so special, both at work and at home. There has been no greater joy than watching my children succeed, each in their own way. And of course, now their children, whom you have gotten to know in the book, are front and center in my life and my heart. They are exceptional kids and have filled our lives with lots of memories and special moments.

Then there is Steve. How lucky can anyone be to have a life partner who shares your ups and downs without complaint? As I have gotten older, I have come to realize how unique our relationship is and how important it is to my life and success. He is a special man, and I hope others can be so fortunate to share a relationship like the one we have built.

Of course, this book is a reflection of lots of experiences that came from knowing and working with some of the greatest people in the world as colleagues, clients, and friends. Thank you all for your trust in me. It is not taken for granted.

The House that Made Me: Writers Reflect on the Places and People That Defined Them, edited by Grant Jarrett. $17, 978-1-940716-31-2. In this candid, evocative collection of essays, a diverse group of acclaimed authors reflect on the diverse homes, neighborhoods, and experiences that helped shape them—using Google Earth software to revisit the location in the process.

Gravel on the Side of The Road: True Stories From a Broad Who Has Been There, Kris Radish. $15, 978-1-940716-43-5. A woman who worries about carrying a .38 special in her purse, nearly drowns in a desert canyon, flies into the war in Bosnia, dances with the FBI, and spends time with murderers, has more than a few stories to tell. This daring and revealing adventured by beloved novelist Kris Radish is her first book of autobiographical essays.

Quiet the Rage: How Learning to Manage Conflict Will Change Your Life (and the World), Richard Burke. $22.95, 978-1-943006-41-0. Where there are people, there is conflict—but conflict divides people. Here, expert Certified Professional Coach R.W. Burke helps readers understand how conflict works, how they themselves may actually be the source of the conflict they're experiencing in their lives, and, most important, how to stop being that source.

A Story That Matters: A Gratifying Approach to Writing About Your Life, Gina Carroll. $16.95, 9-781-943006-12-0. With each chapter focusing on stories from the seminal periods of a lifetime —motherhood, childhood, relationships, work, and spirit—*A Story That Matters* provides the tools and motivation to craft and complete the stories of your life.

ABOUT SPARKPRESS

SparkPress is an independent, hybrid imprint focused on merging the best of the traditional publishing model with new and innovative strategies. We deliver high-quality, entertaining, and engaging content that enhances readers' lives. We are proud to bring to market a list of *New York Times* best-selling, award-winning, and debut authors who represent a wide array of genres, as well as our established, industry-wide reputation for creative, results-driven success in working with authors. SparkPress, a BookSparks imprint, is a division of SparkPoint Studio LLC.

Learn more at GoSparkPress.com